SECESSION

SECESSION

by

MELVIN R. BIELAWSKI

THIS IS THE STORY OF THE SECESSION OF ONE OF THE UNITED STATES FROM THE UNION IN THE 21ST CENTURY. THE RADICAL VIEWS OF MANY GROUPS IN THE UNITED STATES, THE SECRET AGENDA OF ONE OF THE POLITICAL GROUPS, THE MIGRATION OF LEGAL AND ILLEGAL ALIENS INTO THE COUNTRY, THE WIDENING GAP BETWEEN THE RICH AND THE POOR, AND, ABOVE ALL, THE DISSENSIONS OF MANY WITH THE POLITICAL PROCESSES THAT OCCURRED IN THE LATE 20TH CENTURY, WOULD EVENTUALLY LEAD TO THE SECESSION OF ONE STATE FROM THE UNITED STATES.

MELVIN R. BIELAWSKI

ISBN: 1-58721-962-X

1stBooks – rev. 10/31/00

CONTENTS

Page

INTRODUCTION ix

CHAPTER 1
THE BEGINNING OF THE END 1

CHAPTER 2
GROWING PROBLEMS 11

CHAPTER 3
THE GLOBAL ECONOMY 23

CHAPTER 4
NEW POLITICAL PARTIES 33

CHAPTER 5
GROUP X AGENDA--IDENTIFYING CANDIDATE
STATES 45

CHAPTER 6
THE DECISION AND STRATEGY FOR SECESSION ... 71

CHAPTER 7
NEW AMERICA'S MODUS OPERANDI 91

CHAPTER 8
THE IMPACT ON THE AMERICAN CONTINENT 105

CHAPTER 9
NEW AMERICA'S PROBLEMS 113

CHAPTER 10
THE NEW UNITED STATES 119

CHAPTER 11
    COEXISTENCE 127

EPILOGUE.. 133

To Frances

INTRODUCTION

The long range effect of World War II on all of the nations on earth could not even remotely be realized in the immediate postwar years. Boundaries of many nations would be changed, new countries would emerge, some countries would change their names. Economic changes would have dramatic impact on the monetary systems throughout the world. New technologies would revolutionize every facet of the world's population. These and other new developments could not be totally envisioned by the brightest of scholars, scientists, engineers, and politicians of the 20th Century.

The experiences of nations during WW II would function as the stimulus for rapid changes in social, economic, and political systems. As a result, new lifestyles would emerge in the world's population. Many countries would benefit. Dynamic innovations in industry would be dictated by the global markets that would be created via the new nations and desires of people around the world to emulate the lifestyles of the United States and the industrialized countries. The world wide travels of the military during the war and the subsequent business and tourists travel of all people, even from the 3rd world nations, would go far to establish goals for higher standards of living. And, to a great extent, many nations improved the standard of living of their people. Unfortunately, not all nations were able to do so for various reasons. Political corruption, graft, tribal and religious war-fare, nationalism, jealousies, dictatorial leaders and their desire to have their people constantly subjugated would prevent many nations from taking full advantage of the new world order and the global economy. It seemed as though these problems would never disappear from the face of the earth.

Rapid developments would occur in new weapons systems, particularly nuclear weapons. Innovations in energy producing techniques, medicine, space, telecommunications, and data processing would be the direct result of the research and development (R&D) during WW II and continued during the following years.

Some nations continued to be controlled by dictators. Other countries had their political and economic systems controlled by drug trade. In a few instances, both of these elements combined to restrain the growth of some of the nations' economies.

New life styles came into being together with the development of the global economy during the later part of the 20th Century. Simultaneously, diverse political agendas led to the establishment of varied political affiliations and individual initiatives. International and national conflicts were natural outcomes of the dramatic mixing of ideals. The United Nations, born immediately after WW II, received great praise for settling internal conflicts by sending in United Nations troops to keep peace. Such assistance was beneficial in Bosnia and on the African continent.

The United State and the Soviet Union emerged from WW II as the world's two super powers. The coexistence of these two WW II allies during the war years gave way to the so called "cold war" almost concurrent with the end of that conflict. The Soviet threat under Stalin required the United States to not only maintain a large defense posture but to continue to develop new weapons systems. The numerical numbers of the Soviet Union's manpower forces mandated that the United States through high technology build bigger and better weapons. This struggle did cost both nations a great deal of monies that could have been better spent improving the standards of living of the people of the United States and the Soviet Union.

Some scholars believed that the struggle for world domination actually began by the Soviet Union during WW II. Certainly the attempt by Stalin to occupy the entire eastern part of Europe and including the Scandinavian countries was evident in 1945. They did control Eastern Europe including the Balkans until the Soviet Union's collapse in the later part of the 20th century,

Following the end of WW II, the impact of the dynamic issues occurring world-wide and internal to the United States created major social, economic, and political diversities in the United States.

The unexpected demise of the Soviet Union in the 1980's and fall of the Berlin Wall eliminated the largest external problem and pressure on the United States. Reductions in defense spending by both countries and their allies facilitated the revision of their national budgets. The various special interest groups in the United States could focus on their own special agendas.

Pro-choice versus pro-life, immigration, freedom of speech, the right to bear arms, taxes, the right to die, racial and sexual discrimination, and conflicts between ethnic and various religious groups were significant controversies in the later part of the 20th century in the United States. All of these issues and many others were carried over into the early part of the 21st century in the United States. In addition, the division between the two dominant political parties existing at the time, Republicans and Democrats, increased to the point of becoming explosive. All of these factors coupled with the developing global economy and its impact on the working class of the nation plus the lack of any serious international threat to the security of the country, provided a fertile base for the growing discontent in the country.

Few persons, if any, could foresee the events that would occur in the United States in the coming pears. After all, with the exception of a few pockets of unemployment in some sectors of the country, the nation's economy was in good condition, The stock market rose to record high levels., The United States had the strongest military force on earth. What could go wrong? For one, the quest for dominance of ideas would always confront various leaders and special interest groups throughout the world. The United States was no exception.

At the beginning of the 21st century, many of the special interest groups in the United States, some were extremists in pursuing their views, began to become very active in the nation's political arena.

Political candidates were literally forced to rely on the support of various special interests in order to become elected. This strategy applied to local, regional, and national elections. Catering to the special interests became a national disease. It provoked many voters into apathy. Only 50% of the eligible voters in the United States registered to vote. Less than 55% of the registered voters bothered to vote in any local, state, or national elections. Low voter turnout to elections became the norm. Eventually, the elections were controlled by a relatively few groups. This further alienated the population. The agendas of the extremists would become dominant issues at conventions and during elections. Accordingly, groups with opposing views and having their own very special interests in mind became more organized and further diluted the American elections at every level.

New political parties were organized. The United States was no longer dominated by the two political party system.

The United States became a replica of the chaotic political environment of the Central and South American countries of the early 20th Century. This could only develop into a divided nation. The country was facing a crisis on a scale never imagined. It was relatively easy for an extreme group to take advantage of the country's internal turmoil. The culmination of the political chaos would eventually lead to the secession of one of the United States. A new nation would be born as a result of a coalition of certain political forces who were interested primarily in imposing their beliefs and agendas on the American people.

The politically strongest coalition was comprised of the Republican Christian Right and the right to life supporters from various religious, ethnic, and racial groups regardless of their political affiliations; the extreme right wing of the Republican Party, and the various militia organizations located throughout the United States. All of the militias were know as extreme radicals. They were strong for segregation, anti-immigration, and very strong anti-gun control.

Unbeknown to the leaders of this coalition, the extreme right wing and the militia groups had their own secret agenda. The extreme right wing planned to participate in the coalition's objective to select a State for secession and to establish a new nation. However, their own agenda was to establish a nation with a dictatorial government. A government that would not permit any opposing views to their agenda. To the surprise and detriment of the Christian Right and the American people, their efforts would prove successful. This period would prove to be the worst national crisis since the American Civil War that occurred in the 19th century.

CHAPTER 1

THE BEGINNING OF THE END

The United States emerged from World War II (WW II) as the strongest military and economic power on the face of the earth. Its mighty industrial base facilitated the country to produce the necessary weapons to defeat the enemy forces consisting primarily of Germany and Japan. The nation's natural resources coupled with its industrial capacity provided its fighting forces with the necessary tools to win the war.

The nation mobilized quickly after its entry into the war following the attack by the Japanese on Pearl Harbor, December 7, 1941. Shortly after, Germany declared war on the United States. The country united against the common enemy. Even during this period, there did exist major differences among various groups in the United States. For the most part, these diverse groups concentrated on the immediate problem facing the nation, i.e., to win the war.

Racial discrimination was still very strong throughout the land. Ironically it even existed within the nation's military forces during the war. The African-American troops were organized and trained separately. The cities and towns near military posts maintained segregated facilities. Restaurants, toilets, drinking water fountains, public transportation, and housing were racially segregated during and following WW II.

Racial, religious and ethnic prejudice was not unknown. Sexual discrimination existed in the academic and work places. These prejudices took various forms. Job assignments, pay, promotions, and many occupations had built in barriers. Initially, the war did little to change these conditions. However, some subtle changes did begin to take place as the war progressed and the demands of the military services began to deplete the nation's available manpower resources. Due to the labor shortages caused by the build up of the armed forces, many job opportunities were opened to African-Americans and women that were formerly unavailable. As WW II progressed, war

1

production was the top priority. The immediate and common goal of the nation was to win the war. In order to do so, it was mandatory that the nation utilize all of its available manpower resources effectively. The production of war materials and services would take preference over discrimination practises. The United States could not afford to allow any existing prejudices to interrupt its war effort.

During the later part of the 20th century, legal actions and boycotts resulted in Federal laws that prohibited discrimination due to race, sex, ethnic, and religious backgrounds.

The passing of Federal laws did not totally remove discrimination from the American scene, There was little doubt that the laws did assist in decreasing discrimination in the land. There would remain many Americans who would not abide by the laws of the land. There were many who would call themselves religious but who in fact would not honor the decisions of the country's Supreme Court.

The post WW II era, brought economic growth to the United States. The threat from the Soviet Union was the sole major international trial facing the United States in the immediate post WW II years. The disintegration of the Soviet Union in the late 1980's eliminated any serious external pressures on the country. Yes, there were a few relatively minor challenges from various parts of the world, The United Nations (UN), established after WW II, attempted to police the world and prevent a repetition of WW II.

The Middle East was always a potentially explosive area that required the United States and the United Nations to monitor that part of the world via satellites and other means. The United States military forces were always present and on the alert to combat any serious disruption to the world's major oil supplies. The constant threat of Iran and Iraq to produce biological and nuclear weapons posed a significant challenge to the world.

The African continent had its own problems involving tribal and class warfare. The desire for power and control of the various regions necessitated the United Nations to provide constant surveillance and policing of the continent. Hundreds of thousands of Africans perished due to tribal and religious rivalries. If the continent could ever live in peace and form a united front, it would save millions of lives, improve the continent's economy, and raise the standard of living of all its people.

Central and South America had their difficulties. The proximity to the United States permitted economic growth in both areas. Some American businesses relocated their production facilities to the southern States, for example, Alabama, South and North Carolina, Virginia and Tennessee, to take advantage of the lower labor costs. The fact that these were also "right to work" States was also a main attraction. However, many businesses then moved their activities to Central and South America where the wages were only a fraction of those paid in the United States, even in the southern States. This relocation of American businesses to that region did improve the living standards of many in Central and South America. The nation that benefited the most was Mexico. However, the problems associated with the drug cartels and corruption in the governments of Central and South America continued to require the attention of not only the United States but of European countries who were also attempting to establish business activities in those areas. Political corruption and drug trafficking would continue to restrain the area for many years into the future.

The Far East was relatively stable. The nations in the area began to improve their economies and to exist in peace. The free trade agreements permitted the development of industries to provide goods to the United States and the other nations of the world. Some corruption and fraud did pose challenges to certain economies in the area. Their monetary systems were constantly in turmoil. However, these were relatively minor harassments particularly in consideration of the turmoil and suffering that the people experienced in WW II and the immediate following pears.

There did exist other potentially explosive trouble spots, e.g., Cyprus, Bosnia, and parts of the African and Asian continents. The Korean peninsula was a problem due to the conflict between the North and South. The United States and the United Nations

3

were constantly forced to deal with threats to world peace during the late 20th century and the early part of the 21st century.

The tremendous research and development begun in WW II in all major sectors of the United States continued in the post-war years. As a result, the nation developed new technologies in medicine, telecommunications, automation, and in the automotive and aeronautical fields; and, of course, in space exploration and rocketry. Project "Paper Clip", designed to bring into the United States the top engineering talent from Germany after WW II, augmented the nation's top experts in these and other fields of endeavor. The German engineers and scientist contributed immeasurably to the development of new technologies in plastics, light metals, medicines, and ballistic weapons. It was a technical "dream team".

Funds dedicated to research and development by the Universities and Colleges, the Federal Government, and American businesses provided the economic stimulus necessary for growth in the United States into the 21st century. This re-search and development would assure the nation's international dominance in many areas. This would be particularly true in the fields of medicine, space, all phases of telecommunications and automation, robotics, all fields of engineering, and weapons systems. No other nation on earth was able to afford the costs of such extended research and development.

In the 1990's, unemployment in the nation as a whole remained under 5 per cent, In some areas, the rate was less than 3 per cent. Almost everyone who wanted to work had no difficulty in obtaining employment. Businesses were competing for workers,

Some companies developed their own version of the American WW II project, "Paper Clip". They sent recruiting teams to all parts of the globe to hire and bring to this country various specialists, engineers, and skilled employees. Legal and illegal hiring was performed. The laws governing the hiring of illegal aliens were very lenient making the action worthwhile for the employers. After the Soviet Union's disintegration, many of its scientists were available for employment in the United States. The action was advantageous to both nations.

The western countries, i.e., France, Germany, England, Canada and the United States, through democracy, free trade, and economic policies, were the envy of the rest of the world. Other nations began to emulate the West. However some nations were too far behind to take advantage of such development. A division between the have and have-not nations developed. Animosities took root on the international scene.

The western nations in Europe were being over-run by illegal aliens from Bosnia, Africa, and the Eastern countries of Europe. The tide could not be stopped. The European Union permitted free and uncontrolled travel among the member nations. Not all borders were patrolled, As a result, serious economic problems began to develop early in the 21st century. The demands of the immigrants for subsistence, housing, and medical care placed an insurmountable financial burden on the Governments of Western Europe. Central Europe was saturated with millions of illegal aliens. Old prejudices surfaced.

Meanwhile, the United States began to experience its own significant illegal alien problem in the later part of the 20th century. The southwestern part of the United States was the main avenue for hundreds of thousands of illegal immigrants from Central and South America. No amount of manpower and vigilance could control the borders. Corruption of American border patrols contributed to the problem. In addition to the entry of illegal aliens via the southwestern part of the nation, many came from the north via Canada. There were also boat loads of illegal Chinese, Africans, Cubans, people from Vietnam, and other countries from the Far East who managed to come into the country, landing on the uncontrolled shores of the Atlantic and Pacific Oceans and the Gulf Coast.

The Federal Government, due to political advantages, allowed mass legal immigration from the Far East, Bosnia, Eastern Europe, and Central and South America. Many American religious leaders were strong proponents for allowing certain foreign nationals to enter the country, Of course, these were people who shared the same religion or whose conversion was predicated on sponsoring their immigration. This was an era of various racial, ethnic, and religious groups entering the

5

country. Many Americans objected to this influx of such diverse people into the nation's family. This added to the growing discontent with the Government's policies.

The entry of the diverse ethnic and religious groups from the far corners of the earth was some-what akin to the mass legal migrations to this country of people from Ireland, England, and Western Europe in the 19th and early part of the 20th century. Hundreds of thousands migrated to the United States during this period for various reasons. Religious persecutions, poor economies, and the history of wars on the continent were the prime stimulants for the mass migrations.

Copies of ship manifests located in the National Archives in Washington, D.C., recorded the hundreds of ships carrying immigrants from Europe to the United States. The significant difference was that these earlier immigrants were Caucasian and for the most part Catholic or Protestant.

The United States economy provided employment opportunities to all able bodied persons. A labor shortage dominated the market. Employers were hard pressed to fill their vacant positions. The consumer demand for goods and services was so great as to outstrip the suppliers' capabilities. The temptation to hire illegal immigrants by employers was too great to resist. The Federal laws remained lenient. The risk was not great or too expensive if the employer was apprehended. This became an issue with labor unions representing the legal work force.

Due to the successful economy, the labor unions found it extremely difficult to maintain memberships. Recruiting new union members was almost impossible. The majority of the American labor force never experienced the need for unions. The history books contained little data on the 1929-30 recession. Companies in the 21st century had to pay good wages and to provide health and retirement packages in order to retain their labor forces. The competition for labor was too keen for employers to ignore the need for worker satisfaction.

Many American companies, particularly so called mom and pop shops, took advantage of the illegal aliens. Paying lower than the legal minimum wages and no health or retirement benefits was the norm. The illegal immigrants could not and would not complain in view of their status. A "black market" in labor developed.

The diversity of the religions, languages, customs, and social habits of the immigrants in the late 20th and early part of the 21st century were significant. Again, there was the practise of the new immigrants to emulate their predecessors from Europe in earlier years. They would tend to congregate in areas where they could communicate, speak the same language, practise the same customs, and reminisce about their former lands. These enclaves appeared in major cities and suburbs throughout the land. Various ethnic small businesses would proliferate in these areas. Stores that would provide specialties, such as, food, herbs, and other ethnic items were also the gathering places for the customers to meet their friends and acquaintances. Many were homesick for their native lands. They welcomed the opportunity to meet others from their homeland to share stories and speak in their native tongue. If history were to repeat, the next generation would disperse and become integrated within the country.

Education and employment opportunities became the basis for family members' relocations. Distance would separate families and friends.

The nation became seriously divided over many issues during this period. The strains began to show, The country was moving in various directions and seemed to have no central national focus.

The issue of abortions versus pro-life caused major divisions throughout American society. Elements on both sides of the issue became allied with radical groups. The Religious Right was against abortions. As in every movement, fanaticism came into play. Bombing of clinics, murder of medical personnel, and threats to pregnant women who contemplated abortions took place. The pro-life movement became infiltrated with radical right-wing elements. This group certainly was in support of the pro-life movement. But, unknown to the leaders of the pro-life and the Christian Right, the radical right-wing also had other key items on their agenda. These other aspects would eventually surface to the chagrin of the pro-life movement. The anti-abortion movement had the strong support of most Republican politicians and the Republican Party. The Party also attracted the radical right-wing elements of the American political scene. Although few in numbers, the radicals exerted strong influences on the day-to-day operations of the Christian Right and on the Republican Party's agenda. The "right to bear arms" group was also a part of the Christian Right coalition. It was an odd coalition.

In addition, the pro-life advocates attracted supporters from all sectors of the population. Representation from all races, ethnic, and religious groups were counted among supporters.

Those in favor of abortion or freedom of choice as the movement became known, had their own objectives. Basically, they believed it was a woman's right to choose an abortion if she so desired. Historically, this group was not as violent. Although they did have their radical supporters. The Democratic Party was associated with the freedom of choice. Strong support of the woman's right to choose an abortion, came primarily from the women's groups. However, pro-choice, as the movement was also known, did have support from various elements of the population. Its supporters included members from every race, ethnic, and political party in the United States. The number of followers almost equaled the pro-life movement.

The issue of pro-life versus freedom-of choice had split political groups. The arguments, and there were many on both sides of the issue, caused divisions among religious, ethnic, racial, and even family members. The issue, primarily due to its religious implications, would provide the basis for dramatic changes in American politics.

Racial discrimination continued and caused divisions among politicians, businesses, and the general population. The nature of the act was very difficult to establish in certain situations. The subtle practise of racial discrimination took various forms. Although most of the nation and the people believed in equality, a minor portion of Americans would not accept the principle of equality. The immigration of Hispanics, Asians, and people from the Middle East expanded racial discrimination to these groups.

This was nothing new in the history of the country. The early immigrants from Europe had similar experiences upon their arrival in the United States. Of course, none of these groups would ever encounter the nature and scope of discrimination encountered by African-Americans. But, the nation was making the best of the situation. The pro-life and the pro-choice groups accepted support from all racial groups. On the surface, race was not material to the respective cause.

Sexual discrimination became a major issue in the United States in the late 1990's. The nation's armed forces and businesses were challenged on this issue as never before. The pressures on politicians and the courts were continuous. Relief did come much to the chagrin of some groups. It was no coincidence that this issue became a serious challenge to the Christian Right and its right wing supporters. Consideration of the "family" was paramount to both elements.

The immigration issue would not go away. This became more of an issue as time progressed. The country began to see more and more new faces. People with unusual customs and dress became part of the American scene. The various cultures being introduced into the nation clashed not only among groups but also with the established culture which had been in existence in the country for the past century.

All of these issues plus countless others that also existed among the Americans, caused great concern to much of the population. Confusion took control. The commonality that kept the nation functioning during WW II was gone. Deep crevices began to appear that could not bring harmony to the country. The Republican and Democratic Parties became splintered and began to lose their appeal and effectiveness in governing the United States. The radical far right was preparing to take full advantage of the divisions. This was the forerunner of events to come.

CHAPTER 2

GROWING PROBLEMS

Fortunately, there were no major international problems at the beginning of the 21st century. The few minor skirmishes posed no serious threat to world peace. The United Nations (UN) learned its lesson early from its Bosnian experience. In order to preserve the peace, it had to act quickly in dealing with never ending internal revolutions, tribal, religious, and ethnic warfares; threats to neighboring countries, and terrorist activities. Immediate and strong actions by the U.N. was mandatory to maintain world peace. The memories of WW II were still strong and the penalty for procrastination in the face of aggression would take centuries to erase. For the most part the international scene was stabilized by the year 2015. The 21st Century started on a peaceful note.

Bosnia, thanks to the UN, remained quiet. A token force of UN troops was still present to keep the various factions from fighting. The ethnic and religious animosities would remain for many more years. There were signs of mutual trust and respect appearing. This was encouraging to the peacemakers. The belief was that this development, albeit slight, would mature in the coming generations. The significant factor was that there were not the mass killings that took place in Bosnia during the 1980's and early part of the 1990's. The Europeans credited the Americans with taking the initiative to stop the slaughter of thousands of men, women, and children on all sides of the struggle.

The Korean peninsula was united, Communism lost its struggle with democracy. The people of North Korea had extremely difficult times after the breakup of the Soviet Union in the 1980's. The North Korean economy could not sustain itself without the assistance of the Soviet Union and China. Conversely, South Korea developed into a thriving nation beginning with the end of the Korean conflict in the 1950's. The South Korean economy did have its difficulties in the later part of the 1990's. Graft, corporate corruption, and bad business practises almost ruined the nation. They were on the verge of bankruptcy. Thanks to the International Monetary Fund (IMF) and the United States they were able to recoup. Shortly after the turn of the century, the two Koreas united to become one. Their problems would not disappear with the unification. Care had to be exercised to assure that the merger would not cause a financial collapse. The cost of re-building the nation's economy would still require assistance from the International Monetary Fund. The recovery would take time. The Koreans had studied the merger and the problems related thereto of East and West Germany after the collapse of the Soviet Union and the fall of the Berlin Wall.

The lessons learned from the German experience assisted in the peaceful and orderly transition of North and South Korea into a united Korea. Peace was finally a reality.

The Tribal conflicts in Africa were being slowly but peacefully settled. Religious persecutions and prejudice did plague parts of Africa. Mass murders still took place in parts of the continent. The culprit was religious differences between Tribes. There was little the outside world could do to stop the massacres that took place in various parts of the continent. Most of the African problems were confined to North and East Africa. The problems were localized for the most part. There was little danger that the problems would have a major impact on the entire continent and certainly no serious threat to the world. A situation that developed from the internal chaos was the migration of thousands of Africans to central Europe and to the United States. This migration took the avenues of legal and illegal emigrations. The problem was in the masses of Africans who sought to migrate for political and economic reasons and the adverse impact on the economies of the targeted nations. The nations that were involved, their labor unions, and the general populations did not believe that the large numbers of immigrants could be absorbed without serious impacts on the local and national economies. A tremendous strain was placed on the recipient nations. This in turn, caused political problems on a global scale.

Problems of discontent were festering in Central and South America. The economies were very poor compared to the United States. Assistance came in the form of factories that were financed and built by corporations from Europe and the United States to take advantage of low taxes, a large labor supply, and low wages. Even with these conditions, a major portion of the population from the area suffered from unemployment, poor education, and poor health. Many had friends and relatives who had migrated to the United States, legally and illegally, during the later part of the 20th century. The word was passed back to those left behind about the many job opportunities, education possibilities, and health benefits in the neighboring United States. It was no wonder that many would want to emigrate to America and the country with all of the advantages for the families.

The Mid and Far East were experiencing major social and economic problems. Most important, peace was near at hand. The Iraqi leader, Saddam Hussein, was gone from the scene. His death was sudden. The world never learned the cause of his death. It was common knowledge that many of his military were unhappy with the nation's continued struggles with the United Nations. Iraqi's Republican Guard realized that the nation was suffering unnecessarily. The sanctions imposed by the U.N. caused unacceptable hardships on the population.

The nation was in need of medicines, food, and other staples. It was isolated from the business world. It was believed that his top military leaders decided to remove Saddam from the scene. Soon after Saddam's death, the nation began to take its new role as a peaceful nation in stride. The new leaders took advantage of the world's need for oil. It would be only a matter of time before the nation would again become a leader in the Arab world and enjoy a peaceful existence with its neighbors. In time, the past struggles for survival of the people of Iraq would fade from memory.

Iran seemed well on the way to accepting many western customs. Its elite, many of whom were educated in the west, led the nation into the 21st Century. It too, as Iraq, made dramatic changes in its national social and educational policies. It became an active member of the global economic and political scenes.

The Israeli and Palestinian problem was still present. The difficult period of the late 1990's gave way to a more amiable Israeli government at the beginning of the 21st century. There were still serious problems to be addressed. However, the Israelis and the Arab nations, particularly the Palestinians, recognized the futility of fighting each other. It was a period of reconciliation and the acceptance of each other's roles in the region. This development was equal to the tearing down of the Berlin wall in Germany in the 1980's.

There were other problem areas that would continue to fester. The Protestant/Catholic dispute in Ireland, ethnic and religious differences in the Far East, and other comparatively minor clashes would not disappear from the world scene. But, they did not pose a threat to world peace. Fortunately peace was near at hand. The political leaders, encouraged by the United States, continued to make progress toward a lasting peace. There would be elements, however, that would attempt to continue the militant fighting. Lives would still be lost due to irresponsible extremist who would continue to resist a peaceful settlement to the decades old animosities.

The growing internal conflicts of the American people and the general discontent with the political environment erupted into hostile acts within the population. Boycotts and other peaceful demonstrations turned into physical confrontations. The flames of bigotry, prejudice, and anger of the extremists in the nation were being constantly fanned in the media. This was a carry-over from the 20th century. It appeared that few, if any, of the radio talk show hosts of that era were neutral. There were a few radical right wing talk show hosts who were constantly filling the air waves with their own version of bigotry. They were recognized as fanatics. These talk show hosts catered to the extremists in their listening audience.

Some of the television talk show hosts were somewhat neutral. They attempted to provide all sides of the topics. They drew the attention of a large segment of the population.

The average American was saturated with the main issues of the period. It was almost impossible to hear rational arguments on the various subjects of the time.

The Christian Right became dominated by the radical right wing. The Christian Right expanded their own radio and television (TV) shows to proclaim and argue their issues. In particular the right to life and family values were expounded. Unfortunately, the Christian Right talk shows were used by the far right talk show hosts to broadcast their personal agendas. The fact that many of the far right elements' ideas and characteristics clashed with some of the basic principles of the Christian Right posed no serious problem at the time. It was a question of accommodation. This was not entirely unusual. This only reflected the sign of the times. All major political parties and groups would be comprised of supporters with diverse ideas on all of the main issues. However, in the case of the radical right, a secret agenda existed. An agenda that would, when revealed, shock the Christian Right and the people of the United States.

The radical ideas presented by the extremists on all sides of the major issues of the era were endorsed by various political leaders to the detriment of both major political parties, the Republicans and Democrats. The members of both parties became disenchanted with their leadership. The clash of ideas and beliefs began to tear at the basic fiber of their organizations. Against this backdrop, the internal problems in the United States began to come to the surface. The melting pot of the United States began to show strains. The immigration of hundreds of thousands of people from Africa, the Far East, Europe, Central and South America, the Middle East, and from the South Pacific regions created as diverse a population as the world itself. The United States became a nation of many races, ethnic groups, religions, cultures, languages, and political beliefs. This caused major divisions in the population and among the politicians.

The beginning of the 21st century started on a relatively peaceful note. This period of apparent bliss did not last long. By the pear 2020, the minor and nonthreatening issues at the beginning of the century became major threats to the peace and tranquility of the nation.

Minor clashes began to occur in work places, in shopping areas, in neighborhoods, and in church meetings. Opinions were very strong on various topics particularly on abortion; immigration, the right to bear arms, discrimination for any reason, the death penalty, and other constitutional issues.

The nation's immigration policies were attacked by various special interest groups. The immigrants of the past thirty years worked for minimum wages and in some instances for even less than the law required. This posed serious hardships on the families but the immigrants did not object strenuously. Theirs was a far better situation in the United States than what they had left behind in their former homeland. Economically, their standards of living were beyond comparison. The unions could not recruit the immigrants to their cause. The labor unions found allies in some far right elements. This was another situation of accommodating a rival for a common cause. This pattern would prevail throughout the land.

Some of the new immigrants contributed to the problem. Many refused to learn the language. Others refused to show respect for the American flag and the national anthem. Many openly showed allegiance to their native countries. The neighborhoods of many cities began to resemble the later part of the 19th century and the early part of the 20th century in the United States. That was the period of the mass arrival in the United States of immigrants from central Europe. Enclaves, or ghettos, of various racial, ethnic, and religious groups became familiar scenes throughout the land. The new immigrants settled in areas where they could communicate, by using their native language. The new immigrants from Central and South America, Asia, the Middle East, Africa, and the South Pacific areas formed similar settlements or ghettos. As in the previous century, the lack of integration fostered discontent between such groups and the other citizens.

The pro-choice versus the pro-life group became one of the major conflicts in the country. The issue tore apart neighbors and family members. The politicians attempted to study their constituents' thoughts on the subject. Surveys, town meetings, news letters, and every other conceivable means of communication was used to ascertain the voters' preference. The politicians made every attempt to reach the new immigrants. Translators were used to obtain opinions of the people who could vote but not speak the English language. The issue was constantly debated. The politicians had no problem in determining that the entire country was divided on the subject. This determination posed real problems during election periods. The fence had to be straddled. There was no single solution to the dilemma. The political parties accepted strange partners in order to win elections.

Both sides of the topic drew support from elements of the population with which they differed radically on other subjects. For example, the pro-life group embraced the opponents of the nation's immigration policies and those opposed to gun controls. The pro-choice advocates also welcomed into their camp members of these groups.

Verbal conflicts on the issue were common. Physical confrontations became normal. The Christian Right leadership of this period continued with the cause that the leaders of the 21st century began. Even though some of their efforts in business were somewhat questionable from Christian points of view, their political agenda was clear. The pro-life stand would draw followers from all walks of life; various religious and political affiliations, and ethnic backgrounds. And of course there always was the support of the radical right wing.

The main forces of the right to choose, pro-abortionists, were led primarily by women who believed in the freedom of choice. This side of the issue was female dominated. The Democratic Party was aligned with the women's right to choose movement. The followers of this group were politically active and participated in local, regional, and national political election campaigns. They were a strong voice. Their supporters also included some elements of other special interest groups with whom they had major differences, for example, members of the gun lobby and those opposing immigration.

The anti-gun lobby confronted the National Rifle Association (NRA) openly and with strong support from members of both sides of the abortion issue. Conversely, the

NRA obtained the support of many talk show hosts who were on the side of the pro-life issue. This was a strange alliance that was indicative of the times. Americans seemed to becoming a nation of splintered groups, forming alliances without regard for a common agenda.

The issue of the death penalty was another of the controversial issues of the period. Advocates of the death penalty were in conflict with those who opposed capital punishment. The later group was opposed to the death penalty no matter how serious the crime. Those who supported the death penalty were convinced that the only just punishment for capital crimes was death. There were many Americans whose opinions were somewhere in between the two extremes.

The politicians and would-be office holders had a difficult time determining which causes and sides to adopt. The general population was fractured on all major issues. The special interest groups became involved in the local political scenes throughout the nation. No political precinct was taken for granted by any politician. Local knowledge of the voters, organization of the political parties, and assuring voter turn-outs became mandatory to assure victory. Nothing could be taken for granted due to the conflicts that even existed among members of the same family.

Local elections would be used as the base to determine the strategy in state and national elections. One of the main issues to the process became money. The research and analysis plus campaign costs would require unlimited funds.

The laws governing political fund raising were still as nebulous as they were at the beginning of the century. Few, if any, politicians wanted to have stringent controls on fund raising. This lack of control would invite questionable solicitations for contributions by politicians throughout the land. Nothing would change. The two major political parties of the time, Republican and Democratic, were not about to vote for strong controls governing campaign financing.

The relatively new Americans of Hispanic, Asian, African, and European backgrounds became confused over the developments in the United States. All were totally cognizant of the recent clashes between the anti-immigration groups and those who favored opening the country to more immigration. This issue also generated mixed reactions within the Christian Coalition and the Democratic and Republican parties. The relatively few independents in the country fell on all sides of this and the other principle issues. The cracks in the leadership of the various causes and political parties of the nation were becoming clearer and of greater magnitude.

Hispanic-Americans had the strongest representation in the southwestern part of the United States at the beginning of the 21st century. By the year 2020, every state in the union and every major city had increased representation of this group. Their political participation was not limited to local and state elections. Many leaders began to emerge on the national scene. Hispanic-Americans had representation in the United States Congress. A few had served honorably in the various Presidential Cabinets and as foreign Ambassadors. Others occupied postions as Governor and Mayor. Their influence brought recognition to the plight of their fellow Hispanic-Americans who had difficulties in obtaining good educations, employment, and housing.

Based on their numbers and projected family growth, the Hispanic-Americans were projected to be the largest minority group in the United States by the year 2075. This statistic was not lost on the politicians and special interest groups.

The Hispanic-Americans were as susceptible as all other Americans to the pressures from the various special interest groups and to join in whatever causes they sponsored. The result was no different. They became divided amongst themselves on the various major issues facing the nation.

The Asian-Americans, although a smaller minority group than the Hispanic-Americans, settled in various parts of the nation. There were a few enclaves or neighborhoods that were predominantly Asian-American. California and other states on the Pacific coast were favored by many Asian immigrants. Others settled along the Gulf of Mexico coastline. Northern Virginia attracted many Asian-Americans due to its climate.

The Asian-Americans distinguished themselves through their close and strong family ties and their pursuit of education. The

Christian Right endorsed family unity. A bond was established between the two groups. The leadership surfaced in the professional fields. Many joined the medical and scientific professions. Others became leaders in the academic arena.

Their political activities were primarily limited to voting in the elections. Only a relatively few sought political office. Their financial support was sought by all political parties.

The majority of Asian-Americans were very loyal to their new land. Many remembered the difficulties they encountered in escaping from their native lands and the problems they had in becoming legal immigrants. Obtaining American citizenship was their just reward. Only a few were dissatisfied with their American lives. Some maintained close liaison with the homeland. They were confused relative to which country they owed allegiance. This would someday be put to the test.

The African-Americans were a totally different minority group. The main heritage was in the era and times of the slave trade. Their presence in the United States for the vast majority of African-Americans was due to the practise of slavery in the United States in the 18th and 19th centuries. It was not a question of voluntary emigration. Prejudice and racial discrimination was a burden that would stay with them through the centuries. Many would suffer over the years from racial prejudice. Inadequate housing, education, employment, and in every facet of American life including in the military services of the nation would be their constant challenges.

In time, many would rise to national prominence. Leaders would take charge of local and state governments and become prominent in national politics. Others would rise to the highest ranks in the military. Countless others would become outstanding in the fields of education and business. Even in the African-American communities, the national issues would find vast divergence in opinions. In many instances, the differences were extremely radical. The national pattern proved no different with this group of Americans.

There did exist racists, almost unbelievably, among many African-Americans. Some did not advocate integration of the races. Mixed marriages were not supported. There were those who took the side of the pro-life group while others favored the right to choose in the abortion issue. The right to bear arms also found opposite views. The overall make-up of the group was really no different than the rest of the population of the country.

It was no wander that Americans would be establishing boycotts, picket lines, and various demonstrations on these and many other issues. The people of the nation were divided as never before in the history of the country. This was a period totally opposite of the American public during the WW II era: A time when the entire population was united. The ideology of Americans was not dramatically different. This would change in the post-war years, particularly in the 1960's and the American involvement in Vietnam. Major divisions would surface in the country that would tear at the very heart and soul of the nation. The relative peace and tranquility that the nation enjoyed would be lost forever.

CHAPTER 3

THE GLOBAL ECONOMY

The global economy, established during the later part of the 20th Century, specifically in the 1980's and 1990's period, produced a new world order in economics. The major industrial nations of the world, led by the United States, Germany, France, Canada, England, and Japan, began the task of establishing businesses throughout the globe. Corporate actions included relocations of operations to overseas locations that provided lower manufacturing costs. The competitive market dictated decisions that impacted local labor forces, economies, and governments. Concurrently, the fortunate overseas locations were able to improve the standards of living of the local population and establish stability for the area governments. These ventures assisted immeasurably in improving the economies of many nations especially in the third world. The standard of living of the participating nations rose as never before in the history of the world.

American businesses took advantage of the new world markets. Exports reached record levels. At the same time, American businesses were able to import goods produced overseas at much lower costs than in the United States. The various American clothing styles, fast food chains, and other goods and services associated with the Americans were sought by the newly created markets in Europe, the Far East, and other parts of the world. The demands of the American population together with the nation's surge in exports, propelled the country's economy. Employment was at an all time high in the United States. The nation's businesses thrived. Many corporations moved their manufacturing plants from the industrial north and New England areas of the nation to the deep south. The states of Alabama, South and North Carolina, Tennessee, and Virginia were States with right to work laws. Employees did not have to belong to labor unions as did the majority of employees in the north and New England. The

23

southern States also provided tax inducements to corporations, encouraging them to locate to their respective States. Many businesses did in fact move. The so called "smoke stack industries" located in the northern part of the nation were declining rapidly. For the most part, these facilities were obsolete. New industrial plants utilized automation and robotics extensively. High technology began to replace the archaic industries. Downsizing became a common practise.

Thousands of employees were released from the payrolls. These actions caused a tremendous change in the attitudes of older American workers. They were suspect of big business and the government. The turmoil took its toll on the older American families. They were not prepared financially or mentally to retire at the ages of 50 to 60. The government had not yet provided for retraining or other ways to take advantage of this newly business created manpower surplus.

Minor clashes occurred in areas impacted by the plant closings. The objections of labor unions were, for the most part, disregarded by the general public. After all, most Americans did have Jobs. Even so, many American couples had to have two jobs each to make ends meet. Wages for the working class were relatively low.

Eventually, some corporations decided to move their factories and businesses overseas and to Central and South America. These actions would have multiple benefits for the companies concerned. The local populations in the overseas areas would have employment. Their lives would be improved immeasurably. There would not be the need or desire to emigrate to other lands of opportunity. Many would decide to remain in the country of their birth. This in turn would reduce the numbers of legal and illegal immigrants to the United States. This feature was embraced by the far right elements in the country and the labor unions. The down side of the overseas relocations were the numbers of Americans who lost their jobs due to the companies moving their operations overseas. Again an unusual alliance was created between groups with extreme divergent views and goals, i.e., the businessmen and the Republican Party and their far right colleagues and the labor.

As indicated, the down side to these corporate relocations was the obvious impact on the American workers. This was a repeat performance of the earlier moves of companies from the North. The problem would be most acute with the older work force. Employers were not about to hire workers at high wages and who were close to retirement. This pattern repeated itself throughout the nation. A serious division began to develop between the older and younger members of the nation's work force. This combined with the increasing life span of Americans, forced retirements, and growth in high technology widened the gulf between the two age groups.

The global economy was a favorable turn of events for many Americans, particularly the young who were technically trained. The new developments in telecommunications, data processing and transmission, and software created a job market that was previously unknown. The competition for personnel with skills in computer sciences, electronic engineering, and other engineering disciplines was global. Personnel skilled in the technical areas could select their employer, work location, and the nature of their benefits.

Inflation was under control. The prices of consumer goods, for example, automobiles, computers, clothing, home appliances, and food stuffs, remained stable. Many of the products were manufactured in foreign countries. The quality of the merchandise was questionable at times. However, the prices were kept low. Inflation was almost nonexistent.

The Unites States became a service oriented economy at the start of the 21st Century. Almost simultaneously, some light and heavy industry began to return to the national scene. This was due primarily to the tax advantages provided by many states to the corporations, proximity to the American consumers, and the availability of a skilled labor force, This last feature was very critical. Several corporations had quality control problems when they moved their manufacturing facilities outside of the United States. This was especially true for the automobile industry.

The United States took advantage of its research and development in the various fields. It dominated the world markets in many areas. Whether by chance or preplanning, the

American corporations that relocated their facilities to other countries, including the undeveloped nations, created international markets for American exports. With the upsurge in employment and the concurrent income from wages, the purchasing power of formerly poor countries increased dramatically over night. American businesses thrived with the increase in exports. This was a 21st century phenomenon.

Many of the nations depended on American investments to raise their economies. The American dollar became the strongest monetary system on earth. The stock market was supported by the tremendous surge in exports and the influx of billions of dollars of investments weekly from the newly created pension plans of the American workers. This relatively recent savings innovation provided assurance that the United States economy would remain stable. The flow of funds from pension plans and individuals into corporate stocks, bonds, and mutual funds was greater than any time in the history of the nation. Eventually, there would be almost as many mutual funds as corporations listed on the New York stock exchange. Every Friday, literally billions of dollars of 401 (k) and other retirement funds were pumped into the stock market.

With all of the prosperity in the land, there remained some internal pockets of dissension. Older workers had difficulty in obtaining employment. Discrimination still haunted the minorities. African, Asian, and Hispanic Americans still encountered problems in entering certain occupations. The problem was not as severe as in earlier years. But, it was persistent and did cause concern to various state and local governments. The Federal Government enacted laws but it was impossible to have one hundred per cent compliance. Scattered violent demonstrations did not help the situation.

The dominance of the United States in the world economy also caused problems in the international arena. Many nations did not appreciate what appeared at times to be dictatorial terms involving trade. Though the countries had no choice due to their economies being totally dependent on American business, they secretly explored various avenues that would give them more autonomy. Several countries were clearly jealous of the United

States. They did not appreciate being in the position of catering to another country for financial support and stability. Some of these nations were still smarting over their loss of colonies after WW II. Eventually, same of the nations would combine their efforts to control their own economies and destinies.

It was only natural that the Europeans would be the first block of nations to unite and form the European Union (EU). The objectives were long in the making. It took decades to develop. Initially the countries of central Europe, including France, England, a united Germany, Denmark, Austria, Italy, and the BeNeLux came together to debate the forming of the EU. The goals would include eliminating trade barriers and frontiers, establishing a common currency, and sometime in the future, forming a single government. All of these targets would consume a great deal of time. Considering the history of the area, the different languages and customs, the various religious and ethnic groups (especially with the immigrants from Africa, Asia, and the Middle East), the task seemed insurmountable. The initial planning began after WW II. Meetings to discuss the issues were often postponed due to one or more of the nations objecting to the proceedings. Finally, the first stage involving free, unrestricted travel between the member nations began in the late 1990's. This first act brought with it many other unforeseen problems. Illegal immigrants by the thousands began to saturate the EU countries and in particular France and Germany. These two countries had the strongest economies in the EU and were the destinations of choice of many people from the Middle East, Africa, and the eastern countries of Europe. For the most part, these were not refugees escaping from tyranny or persecution but rather people who desired to improve their status in life.

The second important step of the EU was to establish the EU currency in the early years of the 21st century. After many debates and a multitude of arguments, they finally settled on a monetary system that would satisfy a majority of the EU members. As eventful as this was, the action had no immediate impact on the Unites States dollar. Many Europeans would continue to hoard large amounts of United States currency as a form of insurance. Many remembered the numerous problems they encountered with previous currency reforms.

The long delayed but successful implementation of the EU plan did not go unnoticed by the rest of the world.

Middle Eastern countries, with their declining oil reserves coupled with the development of other energy sources by the industrial powers of the west, began exploring the possibilities of establishing a Middle Eastern Union (MEU). Its objectives would parallel the EU. The problems encountered would be similar to some degree.

Different forms of governments, languages, religions, and historical animosities were stumbling blocks to the idea of a MEU. The Middle East nations were more autocratic as opposed to the European countries. This factor together with various levels of oil reserves posed unusual problems for any quick settlements. Tribal jealousy played a major role. There was a sense of urgency in view of the new oil fields that were being discovered and developed in Russia and other parts of eastern Europe. In addition, new oil fields were being discovered in certain parts of Africa and the Far East. These new developments and the use of other energy sources diminished the influence and power of the Middle Eastern block. The power that the area enjoyed in the 20th century was rapidly disappearing.

The Arab world already had an informal unity on such matters as oil production, security of the various States and their relationship with the Israeli nation. This was a basis for a beginning of a more formal union.

The talks of the Middle Eastern nations to form a Union began in earnest in the year 2005. There was little doubt that it would be many years before any viable plan would be developed let alone be implemented. But nevertheless, they did begin. They called upon representatives of the EU and the Americans to assist in the planning.

The action taken by the Middle East to form a Union that would be patterned after the EU, made the nations of the Pacific rim take notice. It was obvious that the nations of Japan, Korea, Thailand, Vietnam, and others in the region needed to form their own alliance. The differences between these nations were so great as to cause years of delay even prior to arranging for meetings on the subject. Cultures, religions, languages, monetary systems, economic conditions, ethnicity, and peoples' attitudes were obstacles that seemed impossible to link. The region was still dominated by problems from WW II and more recent conflicts. The biggest obstacle was the role of China. This was the largest nation in terms of land area and population. This potential market exceeded over one billion people. It would be the controlling force. In addition to having the strongest economy in the area, it was also a world military power. Japan could not match this side of the issue. The area would be stalemated for years to come. There was no hope in sight for the development of a common bond by the nations of the Far East.

The African continent would continue to be divisive. Tribal conflicts were constant. There was no dominant leader in the area to initiate a plan to unite the economies of the various nations on the continent. The gap between the various governments of Africa were the same as existed in the 19th century. Borders were the least of the problem.

Tribal differences dominated the scene. Languages, religions, and the economies of the area differed substantially. But, centuries old tribal differences would linger for years to come. There was no threat to world peace. The terrible internal tragedies were the massacres of hundreds of thousands of Africans by their fellowmen. The world could not control the local fighting. Local governments refused outside aid. The UN was reluctant to introduce forces into an area that had no local support. This chaotic condition would persist even though some of the continent's nations were taking advantage of the new oil fields uncovered by companies from the United States and Europe. This activity added to the continent's problems. The countries that had no oil deposits were jealous and caused still more animosities.

All of these international activities had little impact on the United States. The country's economy continued to grow despite cracks in management/labor relationships. The corporate policies in hiring young workers, employing many part time to avoid paying benefits, reducing the retirement benefits for full time employees; planned downsizing to remove employees from the payroll who were near retirement and older workers who would be replaced by younger and lower paid workers, and other similar corporate actions, persisted.

The division between corporations and the labor unions became intense. Work slowdowns became common. Pickets appeared at the gates, employees argued amongst themselves, the right to work laws were challenged, families and friends argued the pros and cons of unions and the rights of corporations to take whatever actions they deemed appropriate in order to satisfy the stock holders.

In addition to the global economy, other problems in American society caused concern throughout the nation. The abortion issue remained one of the most divisive issues in the country. Violence usually erupted whenever and wherever the issue was discussed. It made no difference if the parties were Christian, Jewish, or any other faith. Race or ethnic background was immaterial. It was the pro-life versus the pro-choice supporters who domineered the scene. Only a relatively small group of Americans, as was the situation with most issues, had no opinion on the subject. There was no majority for or against the issue. Both sides had radical supporters. The feelings and beliefs of the opposing groups could not be settled peacefully. Neither side would relinquish its position. The leaders of both the pro-life and pro-choice movements formed alliances with other American based groups with whom they had diametrically opposing views on many other issues of the period.

The Christian Right did have major support of members from various religious, ethnic, and racial groups. The cause had the support of many members of all political parties. The pro-life issue also attracted many immigrants to the cause. This was due in part to their religious backgrounds. Political support came from many other sources. The Republican Party was on record as being "pro-life".

The pro-life group had the strong allegiance of the radical right wing of the Republican Party. This same group included opponents of gun control and immigration. Above all, the most radical element of the right wing included secret and not so secret State militias whose ultimate goal was to oppose anything and everything that the Federal Government favored.

The extreme right wing were supporters of religious, ethnic, and race discrimination. The Christian Right was not too selective in obtaining support of the pro-life cause. It was a marriage of convenience. However, the ultimate objective of the radical right wing was kept close hold, i.e., top secret. Time alone would reveal their objective. Eventually, the Christian Right would have to pay a very high price for this support. As it developed, the price was too high.

The Christian Right and the pro-life advocates became disenchanted with the Republican Party immediately after the turn of the 21st Century. Too many of the Republican members of Congress were vacillating on the issue of abortion.

The pro-choice issue was dominated by the National Organization of Women (NOW). They too had support from various political, religious, ethnic, and racial groups. As with the pro-life issue, support came from diverse Americans. No doubt the strongest advocates for the right to choose came from women. Their involvement in the American political arena began in earnest in the 1960's and during the Vietnam conflict. The strong surge into politics was really triggered by the abortion issue. The decision of the Supreme Court that gave the women the right to choose an abortion was their major victory that would often be challenged, albeit unsuccessfully, by the right to life advocates.

The abortion issue together with the other internally divisive subjects including immigration, the right to bear arms, freedom of speech, and the ever growing divisions of Americans into racial, ethnic, and political enclaves were the unfortunate mix to cause riots in many parts of the United States. This was tragic particularly in consideration of the peace that was enveloping the rest of the world scene.

Elements of the radical right wing in the country began to realize that the nation was becoming paralyzed within by the recent events. There was little doubt that the items on their agenda could be pursued successfully unless dramatic changes would take place in the political process.

The small and elite group of the Christian Right and radical right wing of the Republican Party met in Charlottesville, Virginia, in the summer of 2007 to evaluate current events and to develop a strategy for accomplishing their agenda. This secret meeting would have a historical impact on the United States.

The attendees at the meeting agreed to maintain a solid front on the pro-life issue. This would assure support from many segments of the American population. Other issues, such as immigration, discrimination, gun laws, and similar topics would not be in the forefront of the Republican Party. Controversial issues would be tabled. The strategy was to gain the political support of the nation's most significant issue, pro-life.

It was agreed that once the Party gained control of Congress and the Office of President together with most State Houses and Governorships, the Christian Right would establish a new national political Party to maintain its ideals. The Party would be called, "The Christian Coalition Party".

The next and most daring step to be taken would be for the Christian coalition to develop a strategy for selecting one of the United States to secede from the Union. A new, democratic nation would be established to foster and maintain the ideals of the Christian Right.

In 2024, the Christian Coalition Party took control of most State offices, the United States Congress, and the Office of President. The first major objective became a reality. The stage was set for the next major action. The strategy was proceeding without any major setbacks. The radical right wing members of the coalition were overjoyed at the pace of developments. They played their part in the various business meetings well enough to earn compliments from the leadership of the Christian Coalition.

The President of the United States was a hand picked man who was literally a pawn of the Christian Coalition. It was no secret that he did not make any major decisions on foreign or domestic policies without the approval of the Head of the Christian Coalition and his two principal subordinates. The latter were connected directly to the radical right wing.

CHAPTER 4

NEW POLITICAL PARTIES

During the organization of various regions of the world into economic and political alliances for survival in the global economy, the various divergent groups in the United States became frustrated with their inabilities to enforce their beliefs on the nation. With the economic growth of the United States there also developed a restless era. Internal differences dominated the political scene. These differences were numerous and significant.

The Christian Right with its emphasis on the anti-abortion issue or pro-life as its cause became known, was very frustrated with its inability to sway the majority of Americans to its views on this subject. Their principal support came primarily from fellow Christians and also members of other religious groups. Support for the pro-life issue also emanated from several organizations that had radically opposing views on other important topics of that period. For example, the gun lobby, anti-immigration backers, and the armed militia groups that materialized in many of the States since the end of World War II (WW II). By far, the most controversial supporters of the Christian Right and its pro-life stance was the radical right wing of the Republican Party. It was this alliance that would bring unforeseen troubles to the United States.

The beginning of the 21st Century bode serious problems for the United States.

The pro-life advocates included members of every religious, racial, and ethnic segment of the country's population. Their protests took them to all of the State capitals in the country. Organized and mass demonstrations took place in the nation's capital, Washington, D.C. Some of the activists became overly aggressive. Zealots would take control of the marches. What began as peaceful marches turned into riots. It was necessary on several occasions for some Governors to bring out the National Guard to control the crowds. The leadership of the demonstrations lost control of the meetings. Chaos reigned in the United States.

There was some indication that the riots were initiated by the radical right wing of the nation. Radio talk show hosts, through their dialogue, encouraged confrontations not only with the police but with the "right to choose" or "pro-choice" groups. Many supporters of the pro-life marches blamed the confrontations on supporters of the right to choose. It was true that the pro-choice supporters did confront the pro-life matchers. However, these were peaceful confrontations. There was evidence suggesting that the extreme right wing elements created these disturbances to gain publicity for the cause and to sway public opinion.

The radical right wing of the Republican Party, most of whom were strong supporters of the pro-life issue, also included members who were against immigration and gun control. This was the arm of the Republican Party that attracted the segregationists, the armed militia groups throughout the United States who advocated violence against the Federal Government, and others who supported the right to bear arms. It was a strange alliance indeed. The various factions that comprised the groups that supported the pro-life issue grew in numbers over the years. This growth facilitated the backers to control the elections in many cities and states in the country. The control of the national elections by the Christian Right and their allies would become a reality in the Presidential elections in the year 2012. All of the candidates who were endorsed by the pro-life supporters won local, state, and national elections. The strategy developed in Charlottesville in 2007 was realized.

Initially, the "right to choose" supporters had victories through the Federal court system. Their support came mainly from women and the National Organization of Women (NOW). However, they also had support from members of both the Republican and Democratic Parties. The Democratic Party was a strong backer of the right to choose. As in the case of the right to life, support for the cause also came from various religious, racial, and ethnic groups. The American society was truly splintered on the abortion issue.

Many proponents of immigration, integration, and gun control were also counted in the numbers supporting the right to choose. The bombings of clinics and murder of medical persons involved in performing abortions attracted many supporters who were otherwise neutral.

The other major issues of immigration, integration, and gun control would not disappear from the American scene. To the contrary, the arrival in the United States of thousands of illegal and legal immigrants during the period of 1980 through 2010 exacerbated the immigration problem. Due to the labor shortage in the nation, many businesses were eager to hire the immigrants, illegal or legal. It did not matter. The immigrants worked hard to earn their wages. They were happy to be in a land where they enjoyed freedom. The monies earned were shared with their families in their native land.

Businessmen enjoyed having the immigrants. They were a good labor supply. The demands of the immigrants were unlike those of the native Americans, particularly the union employees. The real important advantage was the low wages they paid to the immigrants. Plus, the businesses did not have to pay for special benefits, such as, health insurance and retirement. Of course, the illegal aliens could not complain. Besides, they were happy with the pay. The profits of the businesses employing the foreigners were outstanding. This was particularly true for the small businesses. Both parties were very satisfied.

The arrival of immigrants from Africa, Asia, and the Middle East added to the racial diversity in the country. Immigration of people from Central and South America provided the nation with the largest minority group. They would replace African-Americans as the dominant minority group in the country by the year 2050.

All of these groups had experiences with discrimination. It was no wonder that many would support the cause of NOW. In many instances, the issue caused disruptions in family harmony. It was not unusual to see several Asians or Hispanics in a boisterous argument on the issue of abortion. Members of the other races and ethnic backgrounds were no different. In many respects, these groups represented average Americans. They too were divided on the main issues facing the nation, particularly the abortion issue.

Other advocates of pro-choice came from the ranks of the gun control groups i.e., those who favored strong gun control laws. Although a relatively small group, they were able to use their leverage at election times. Their strength was in being able to obtain support for their cause in exchange for supporting candidates of the pro-choice stance at election time.

The subject of integration, particularly in the African-American community, was most important. The struggle for equality was still ongoing. Much progress had been made in this area, especially since the late 1990's. However, most everyone recognized that there was still a long way to go to level the playing field. But here also, a dividing force existed within the African-American community on the subject of abortion. There were many who were pro-life. There were also many supporters of pro-choice. And, as with other national groups, there were those who were neutral and took no side of the argument. There were also African-American supporters and dissenters of immigration and gun control. None of the racial or ethnic groups in the Unite States were 100 per cent in agreement on any of the major issues facing the nation.

The political arena grew wild. Professional politicians did not know which sides to cultivate. The various special interest groups were constantly demanding their services and support. The Republicans and Democrats were finding that the issues confronting the nation were literally tearing the Parties apart. Political rallies turned into chaotic, uncontrolled scenes. The leaders of the rallies lost control over the audiences. The attendees argued vehemently over the issue of abortion, immigration, gun control, and foreign trade. More often than not, the meetings erupted into physical violence. This could be predicted. It became impossible to have peaceful meetings and discussions on any of the major issues. There was always the "other" critical issue, discrimination. Although not specifically addressed, there were many underlying factors in contributing to the general public's unrest.

The leaders of both political parties were faced with a monumental dilemma, They had to request police presence at all scheduled political meetings. It was as though a terrible sickness overcame the American public. There appeared to be no solution to the problems. Civility became unknown.

This development did not go unnoticed by the leaders of the "right to life". Their faith in the Republican Party was somewhat shattered. The chaos of the politicians was obvious. The agenda of the Christian Right would not be totally endorsed by any existing political party due to the divisions and the issues within the Parties and the nation and the wide diversity of opinions. However, the leaders of the Christian Right did recognize that their causes, considering the alliances, attracted a large portion of the American population. These numbers could be translated into "voters". This was a very critical and significant observation. It was a fact that the Christian Right would need to capitalize upon. The elections of 2012 proved their strength.

In 2020, the Christian Right leaders and supporters of the right to life invited key members who also supported this issue from the various other religious, ethnic, racial, political and even far right groups to a meeting in the nation's Capital, Washington, D.C. A motel was reserved to accommodate the session. The subject of the meeting was addressed in the announcement as "The Right to Life". The real purpose of the Christian Right was to establish a new political party in the United States, the "Christian Coalition Party" (CCP). This new political party would embrace, at least on the surface, the issues of pro-life, family values and integrity, immigration, anti-discrimination, the right to bear arms, and tougher laws for all major crimes. The meeting was very successful. All attendees fully endorsed the idea of a new political Party.

The national political leaders who attended, primarily members of the far right from the Republican Party but also a few members of the Democratic Party who were know to be sympathetic to the right to life issue, embraced the objective of a new political party 100 per cent. From their perspective, this would provide the strong base for assuring that they would be reelected and at the same time parallel their own beliefs on the main issues of the period.

Within days, the group began to develop the ground rules of the CCP. The plans that would outline the necessary procedures for the Party organization were developed. Within weeks of their first meeting, the Christian Right leadership established the rules to govern the operations of the CCP. The group had the advantage of receiving drafts of the documentation prepared by the Christian Right even prior to the conference in anticipation of events.

On July 4, 2020, the Christian Coalition Party was born. The movement grew rapidly to the amazement of the coalition leaders. This was the first significant new political Party in the United States in over one hundred years.

The impact of this development was not lost on either the Republican or Democratic leadership. The die was cast to bring dynamic changes to the American political scene. Both political Parties were fully cognizant of the action. The radical right wing of the Republican Party knew what was happening. They were in meetings with the leadership of the Christian Right at the embryonic stage of the idea in Charlottesville in 2007. However, it would be devastating to the Republican politicians who tried patronizing their constituents without taking strong positions on the right to life issue and the other far right causes. They were devastated by the developments. They could only hope that the majority of their constituents would not desert the party.

The impact on the Democratic Party was not as devastating. At least not yet. Time to digest the developments and to study how the new political Party would effect the elections was required. However, there was some sense of urgency. Elections always came too fast. The Presidential elections of the year of 2024 would be unforgettable. The Party leaders recognized that the new Party would attract many from the Democratic ranks. The only question that remained was in what numbers?

There was little doubt that the demise of Republican and Democratic Parties, as know in the past, was a forgone conclusion. Those politicians clinging to the old views were in trouble, They could only hope that the majority of their constituents would not abandon them. Theirs was a totally unrealistic view of the developing events.

The political right wing was elated with these developments. They would have the best of both worlds. The political leaders in this group were astute enough to realize that they would be in position to garner support from various sources.

They would certainly have the total support of the nation's voters who favored the right to life. Support would also come from many Democrats, Republicans, and members of the far right, including the various militias located throughout the United States. Additional support would come from the various racial and ethnic groups who were historically associated with the Democratic Party.

The CCP began in earnest to gather supporters and financial contributors to their cause. They established their headquarters in Richmond, Virginia, a state that had already elected local and state officials who endorsed the CCP ideas.

These unexpected and rapid developments, had a profound impact on the pro-choice advocates of the abortion issue. A crisis was at their door. The proponents of pro-choice realized that if they were to maintain the nation's laws on the subject, they would have to organize politically to counter the challenge from the CCP, strong advocates of the right to life. The leaders of pro-choice began to study the strategy employed by the right to life advocates. They soon learned of the organization and policies adopted by the CCP. There was no doubt that the new Party had the support of a variety of groups that were incompatible on some issues but were in favor of the right to life ideas, the principal issue and the foundation of the CCP Party.

The struggle of the pro-choice advocates to build an organization in support of their cause was not going to be an easy task. NOW was the base of the pro-choice movement. They would have to take actions similar to the pro-life backers if they were to continue to be capable of sustaining their movement. Their challenge was far greater than the pro-life supporters. They could not garner the support of a large variety of groups as the pro-life proponents. They were, however, able to attract some supporters from the various racial and ethnic groups and from the new immigrants.

The greatest challenge to the pro-choice group was to decide if they too should organize a new political party. After a meeting of the main backers of pro-choice, it was determined that their cause would attract more support if they would also establish a new political Party. They recognized that many Democrats had abandoned the Party to join the Christian Coalition Party (CCP). The thinking was that perhaps the pro-choice movement would be able to proselytize members from both the Republican and Democratic Parties to their cause. They proceeded on that assumption. At a meeting of the pro-choice national leaders in Chicago, it was decided that a new political party would be formed, called "Freedom Party", or "FP". A national organization was established.

The FP developed its own modus operandi and governing procedures. In essence, the FP had only one major issue, pro-choice. Other aspects, such as, immigration, gun control, the environment, and discrimination were also contained in the Party's platform but at a lower priority. This would prove to be a major miscalculation that would haunt the Party in all elections. The FP was formally established on June 1, 2021. Their national headquarters was established in Chicago.

The chaotic trend in politics continued unabated. Many members of racial minorities and ethnic groups were fully cognizant that neither the FP or CCP fully recognized their plight in the United States. These groups also had support from some liberal organizations who were in total sympathy with their views. In the year 2023, representatives of several minority groups met with a few leaders of various national organizations. The objective was to consider establishing a political Party whose main supporters comprised members of minority groups. The difficulties encountered in this effort were totally unlike the pro-life and pro-choice advocates. The problems of various languages, cultural differences, and in most instances radical religious beliefs and practises would need to be overcome. This would be no easy undertaking. The action would require outstanding skills in diplomacy and organization. The organizers would have to tap the various foreign language media throughout the nation. Representatives of the movement would be required to visit the leaders of the many ethnic and racial organizations in order to gather support and to expound on the benefits to be derived from forming their own political Party. No doubt the Party so organized would be small in terms of numbers. The objective would be to provide support to larger Parties on the various political issues. Basically, to provide the pivotal votes to swing the elections. By the end of 2023, the new political Social Scientist Party (SSP) was established. The supporters represented various labor groups, African and Asian-Americans, Hispanics, and voters who were disenchanted with the overall American political scene.

The establishment of Christian Coalition Party, Freedom Party, and the Social Scientist Party caused havoc within the Republican and Democratic Parties. The leadership of both Parties were appalled at the turn of events. For all practical purposes, these Parties would find it almost impossible to sustain operations. The leaders of both of these Parties kept clinging to the hope that the past events would reverse themselves. They sincerely believed that the new political organizations could not survive and would eventually disappear from the American political arena. This was not going to happen. At least not for the foreseeable future.

The national elections of 2024 would make believers of all of those politicians who doubted the strength and versatility of the new players in American politics. The Christian Coalition Party, with the support of the Republican Party, took control of Congress and the Office of President.

With the Congressional and Presidential victories in the 2024 elections, the first target established by the elite CCP group in Charlottesville in the summer of 2007 was achieved.

The national elections that took place in the year 2024 reflected the history of European elections. Coalitions of the various political Parties was necessary for any Party to control the States and national offices, including Congress and the Presidency.

The primaries and conventions that preceded the elections of the year 2024 surfaced the reality of the chaotic situation that was the direct result of the new political Parties. In previous years, the Democratic and Republican Parties dominated the election scenes. True, their support emanated from the various diverse groups that would eventually turn their support to the new parties. But, the election process was relatively quiet and orderly. Certainly there were some side shows. A few squabbles erupted and some physical encounters occurred. But overall, the process was relatively peaceful. A new era unfolded in American elections. None of the political parties including the CCP, were happy with the turn of events.

The Christian Coalition Party (CCP) was disappointed with the election results. Although the Party was by far the most popular in the nation, it had to depend on a coalition with the Republican Party to take power and control of the various State and national offices. The CCP was also supported by the most extreme and radical groups in the nation, including the various State militias. This did not sit well with the Christian Right, the principal leaders within the CCP. The fact that the CCP had to submit to concessions to the Republican Party and the extreme right wing in order to maintain their agenda did not please the CCP hierarchy. Based on the strategy of the CCP elite group in Charlottesville, their next step would be to establish a new nation at the expense of the United States.

The leaders of the Freedom, Social Scientist, and Democratic Parties could not muster a strong enough coalition to control the elections. They did, however, gather adequate political support to have some of their candidates elected to local and State offices. Also, they were able to have representation in Congress. The struggle for power would continue. The diluted power resulting from five versus two political parties would be detrimental to the nation.

This American phenomenon was observed by the rest of the world with more than just a passing interest. America's dominant role in military and economic affairs has been unchallenged for the last fifty plus years. Europe, Asia, the Far East, and the Middle East were totally unprepared for the dramatic events occurring in the United States. The world soon reacted with sharp drops in the stock markets. The dollar was used in many countries as the monetary system of choice. All of the nations and foreign exchanges would be watching the American scene with suspicion. The big question on their minds, and with many Americans, was what impact would the new developments in American politics have on the world's economy?

It would be many years before this question could be answered intelligently. In the interim, it would remain a puzzle.

The most dramatic action to be taken by the CCP, to establish a new nation from one of the United States, still remained on the agenda. It appeared to be an insurmountable task.

There would be no doubt that the world would be shaken by the coming events. No one, not even the leaders of the CCP, could imagine the impact that such an action would have on the United States, national and international politicals, the world economy, and world peace.

The leaders of the extreme right wing of the CCP and their counterparts in the Republican Party kept a low profile. They could afford to wait for the final act. Their opportunity to achieve their goal would materialize sooner than expected. Secret plans continued to be developed that would be implemented upon the CCP's successful action to have one of the United States secede from the Union.

CHAPTER 5

GROUP X AGENDA--IDENTIFYING CANDIDATE STATES

The Christian Coalition Party (CCP) viewed the 2024 national elections as successful with many reservations. They realized that their power was contingent on support from outside its ranks. A review of the 2024 election returns indicated that of all of the political parties, i.e., Freedom Party (FP), Social Scientist Party (SSP), Democratic Party, the remnants of the Republican Party, and their own CCP, the CCP garnered the most votes. However, they did require support from the Republican Party to win the State and national elections. This factor convinced the CCP hierarchy that their second goal established at the meeting in Charlottesville, in the summer of 2007, was the proper next priority.

The next goal of the CCP would test its political support, organization skills, and dedication to its cause. To select a State for seceding from the United States and establishing a new Democracy on the shores of North America would be an enormous undertaking. Failure could result in a catastrophe for the CCP and its leadership. Success would be glorious.

In September, 2025, the CCP designated a select group comprised of six leading members of the Party to develop the plan that would result in one of the United States seceding from the Union. This working group of six became known as "Group X". The six members included three individuals from the extreme radical right wing of the CCP and the Republican Party. This was not by accident. The radical right wing of the Republican Party had its own agenda. The seceding State would become a new nation and would be politically controlled, at least in theory, by the CCP. This action would facilitate the CCP exercising total and independent control of its ideals in the new nation while still maintaining a strong presence in the United States. The Party would use its strength in the United States to support the secession. This was the strategy of the head of the CCP. However, the secret agenda of the extreme radical right wing of the Party would eventually surface to the chagrin of the CCP.

The charter of Group X called for secret sessions to be conducted at a private hunting lodge in central Idaho. The State of Idaho was selected for several reasons. It was well known that the State had radical right wing groups, including a heavily armed militia. The State and area were sparsely populated. Past elections reflected the voters' favorable attitudes toward CCP ideas. There were no recent events that would attract attention of the general public to the State.

The Group would have three months to analyze and recommend which of the United States should be targeted for secession. The report would be submitted on January 1, 2026, to the head of the CCP who in turn would submit it to the special panel consisting of the head of the CCP and two principal officers for review and implementation. Through collusion, the radical right wing was able to have two of its own followers joining the head of the CCP. They would have the power to reject the report as written or implement the recommendation with any modifications they deemed appropriate. This task would be accomplished by February 1, 2026.

The report developed by Group X would include but not be limited to the following:

1) The State to be targeted for secession and the rationale. The rationale to be in depth.
2) The specific actions to be taken by the CCP in order to accomplish the deed in totality, and
3) A detailed time frame for the actions to be taken by the CCP.

The head of the CCP had no idea of the ultimate intentions of the extreme radical right wing supporting the Party. The participation of the three right wing members was engineered from the outset. Everyone was aware that there were radical elements of the CCP who had extreme views on such items as the right to life, immigration, gun control; discrimination of various racial, ethnic, and, ironically, even certain religious groups. By far the most extreme right wing supporters were the armed militias scattered throughout the country. The armed militias were the most dangerous segment due to their own secret coalitions and ambitions. The right to life cause linked a very strange assortment of supporters. Many of the right to life supporters cringed at the thought of sharing their efforts with extremists. It really was a choice, in their minds, of the lesser of two evils.

At the beginning of October, 2025, the six members of Group X convened in the private hunting lodge to begin their task. It would be no easy undertaking. The group requested and obtained volumes of reference data. Maps and land data were obtained from the Library of Congress. Census data for the past fifty years was obtained from the Census Bureau. Other information was received from the Commerce Department. Every conceivable type of information pertaining to every State in the nation was obtained for consideration by the Group. Ironically, most of the material came from the various Federal Offices in the nation's capital, Washington, D.C. In addition, volumes of other reference material, such as, the Book of Knowledge, Encyclopedia Britannica, and other commercially produced information that contained important and critical data on voting records, education levels, commerce, budgets, and ethnic and religious make-up of each State that would enter into the decision process. The daily schedule of Group X consisted of eating, sleeping, and working on the plan. The lodge had simple but functional furnishings. The provisions were more than adequate. There were ample supplies of food including fresh fruits and vegetables. Liquid refreshments were in the form of soft drinks and fresh water. There was no alcohol or television. This was to prevent and minimize any possible distractions. A telephone was installed that was to be used only for emergency outside calls. The Group was told not to expect any incoming calls unless of an extreme emergency nature. In addition, if the phone did ring they were not to answer the phone until the fourth and last ring. This would be followed by a legitimate phone call from the CCP. This provision was made to assure that only calls from the main office of the CCP would be incoming. This was to negate any possible information leaking out of the CCP that would lead to the news media, or any other unwanted source, from contacting the lodge. Thus, Group X began its work. The strategy of the CCP took a giant step forward.

The first two weeks of the Group were occupied with becoming organized, reviewing all of the reference materials, developing their time schedules, and completing the task of narrowing the list of States to be selected for an in depth review of which one should be targeted for secession.

The Group's first action was to determine the geographic area of the United States to be targeted. Consideration was extended to several factors that were critical if the secession was to be successful. No detail was to be ignored.

The State selected would have the reputation of being sympathetic to the main themes of the CCP. Previous elections of the States would be reviewed to ascertain the history of voters. How many of the State's eligible population were registered voters? How many voted in the previous three national elections? Did they vote Republican or Democrat? Was there political support for the main themes of the CCP?

The reputations and attitudes of the neighboring States of the State selected would be important. If the neighboring States had reflected support in the past of the Christian Right and the right wing causes, the nation as a whole would more than likely accept the action. A critical item considered essential by the group was access to the outside world, both by sea and sir.

Based on these considerations, the group began in earnest to study the map of the United States. With the criteria for the state to be selected requiring access to the outside world, this appeared to be the easiest task in the process. Having a large map of the United States hanging on the wall of the lodge, the group was able to address the entire country.

The Group considered the States of Alaska and Hawaii prior to addressing the contiguous United States. Their rationale was based on several factors. First and foremost, both States had established records of firm voting. Hawaii was considered

48

strongly Democratic. Alaska had voted solid Republican for the past thirty years. Both were off-shore, i.e., outside of the lower 48 States. No buffer States existed for logistics and other support that might be required. The CCP did have substantial support in both States. The Group considered Hawaii and Alaska as high profile States. That is, both were believed too important to the United States to lose for any cause. The States also attracted great numbers of tourists. This was not desirable from the secessionists point of view. All of these considerations were documented for inclusion in the Group's report to the CCP scheduled for January 1.

The second group of States to be crossed off of the map as candidates for secession were all of the States that were bordered by other States and having no access to the seas. Air access was too limited and subjected to restrictions. States such as Kentucky, Arkansas, West Virginia, Kansas, Iowa, South Dakota, Nevada, Arizona, and Wyoming were dropped from consideration without too much deliberation. The Group did recognize that some of these States did have well organized and strong militias and extreme right wing elements. Several of the States were historically strong Republican. These aspects were considered very desirable by the Group. But with the other key factors to be considered, the Group proceeded to drop the States from consideration.

The next geographical area studied by Group X were the States bordering Canada and the Great Lakes. The States adjacent to Canada, such as, Idaho, Montana, North Dakota, Vermont, and Minnesota were dropped from the list of candidate States for two reasons, They did not have access to the seas and many of these States were bordered by neighboring United States that were not in total sympathy with the CCP ideals. Also, Canada's political relationship with the United States would make it an unreliable and unsympathetic neighbor. This factor could be negated if the neighboring States were pro-CCP and, in the case of Canada, the Canadian States were believed to be sympathetic to the idea of separatism. An example of the latter, would be Quebec, Canada. The new nation would need a friendly environment.

Also eliminated were the States bordering the Great Lakes.

The Group took into consideration the Saint Lawrence Seaway. However, they determined that this waterway was too limited. States such as Ohio, Michigan, Illinois, Wisconsin, Pennsylvania, and others bordering the Great Lakes and Canada would have limited and controlled access to the outside world. All of these midwestern States were deleted from consideration. Thus far, the task of narrowing the choice of States to be considered for secession was relatively easy. This was due to the established requirements of the Group for a State to be favorably considered.

It was obvious by looking at the map of the United States hanging on the wall of the lodge that the States to be considered by the working Group for secession were the States bordering the Pacific Ocean, the Gulf of Mexico, and the Atlantic Ocean. These State had access to the outside world via the seas and airports. Recognizing that there was the possibility of blockades, the Group decided that the problems of the United States would be more difficult to enforce blockades on the high seas and in the air of these States.

Twenty one States would be seriously studied in the next several weeks for the dubious distinction of becoming a new nation on the American continent.

The States of Washington, Oregon, California, Maine, Massachusetts, New Hamshire, Rhode Island, Connecticut, New York, New Jersey, Delaware, Maryland, Virginia, North Carolina, South Carolina, Georgia, Florida, Alabama, Mississippi, Louisiana, and Texas would be put under a microscope. Every conceivable feature would be analyzed with particular emphasis devoted to their past voting histories, recent census data identifying the population figures, current and past political leanings, economic factors, and the political leanings of neighboring States. The one very important feature that these States had in common was access to the sea. The group decided that the Pacific coastal States would be the first to be addressed. This appeared to be natural if for no other reason than numbers alone. The experienced gained would be beneficial in reviewing the Atlantic and Gulf States.

The discussions, pros and cons of each State, would consume the Group for weeks. The influence of the three radical right wing members would dominate the dialogue and final decision. The number of hours in meetings meant nothing. Night and day were commingled in the sessions. No one kept track of the hour or day. The time passed rapidly.

The first State to be addressed by the Group was Washington. The factors in favor of targeting the State were many. It had access to the outside world via air and sea. The State had a recent reputation for being pro-life and having right wing leanings. Based on recent census and other public information data, the voters favored the Christian Coalition Party. The State's population was approximately six million and growing. It was no secret that the State had strong support from some extreme right wine elements. There were many in the State who were anti-immigration. Many believed that the United States should change its immigration policies. Many wanted the United States to stop all immigration. The majority of the recent immigrants were from the Far East. They numbered in the tens of thousands. The racial and cultural differences between the immigrants and the native Washingtonians began to surface at the turn of the century. There was no indication that the clashes were about to subside.

Most of the native population were outdoorsmen. They enjoyed hunting and fishing. It was no wonder that they also opposed anti-gun laws. An item that Group X believed to be very significant was the number of eligible voters versus the number who actually voted in the recent national elections. The number of eligible voters was approximately 2.5 million. This represented roughly half of the population of the State. Of great significance was the number who voted. Less than half of the eligible voters actually voted. This suggested apathy on the part of the voters. In terms of CCP strategy, it also suggested that the State would probably be an easy target for manipulation. Bluntly speaking, it would pose no problem for the CCP to gain control of the political offices in the State of Washington.

A factor that also was of interest to the Group was its proximity to the State of Idaho. Elements of the extreme radical right were located in Idaho. The area of Coeur d'Alene, located in northwestern Idaho, had a population in excess of 25,000 inhabitants. Many of the inhabitants were known to be supporters, if not members, of an armed militia. There were a minimum of three known militias in Idaho. It was also known the militias were interconnected organizationally.

Some of the factors that involved the State of Washington were considered detriments. The population of approximately six million was considered somewhat sizeable for the undertaking. The fact that the population did have relatively very strong leanings toward the causes of the CCP made it a strong candidate to remain a part of the United States in order to support the secession in Washington, D.C. The secession of a State would be a major concern of the power structure in the nation's capital. The CCP would need to have support from within the nation if the action was going to be successful. Group X believed that the CCP could depend on its followers in the State to support its ultimate goal.

Of concern to the Group was the neighboring State of Oregon. True, the State was neutral on the pro-life versus pro-choice issue. However, it did lean politically to the Democratic Party. The question of how much support the State would provide to the CCP cause could not be answered due to many variables in the equation.

With all of these factors digested, it was decided to identify the State as an undesirable candidate for secession from the United States. It was not considered an ideal prospect.

Group X determined that the various factors considered in evaluating the State of Washington would also apply to the other eighteen States to be analyzed.

Oregon would be the next State to be studied by Group X for possible targeting for secession. It was already determined that the State's voting history was pro-Democratic. This was a negative point at the outset. Having a history of leaning toward the Democratic Party would make it an uphill battle for secession. Although the State did have some attractive features from the Group's point of view.

Oregon had a population of slightly over three million, The number was considered within the ball park for a State to be targeted for secession. It did have a relatively high number of eligible voters and people who actually voted. Roughly sixty percent of the State's eligible voters were registered. Of this number, approximately sixty-five percent actually voted in the past four national elections. These figures would be considered low by foreign countries. However, based on all of the United States data, the figures were above average. This was of course an indictment of voter apathy in this country.

Oregon had many other attributes. Its education system was considered better than average. The State provided a friendly family environment. It had diverse industries consisting of mining, timber, fishing, light manufacturing, and tourism. Some farming, including dairy farms, was also found in various parts of the State. Most of the farms were owned by fourth generation Americans. The original owners were immigrants from Germany and the Scandinavian countries.

The State's population was composed primarily of native born Americans. The influx of immigrants since the turn of the century, primarily from the Far East, was not significant. This was attributed to the lack of employment opportunities.

Oregon did have access to the Pacific Ocean. Portland could also provide air access to the outside world. Its neighbors, Washington and Idaho, were pro-right. However, the same could not be said for its neighbor to the south, California.

The State was known to have tight internal circles. There were several supposedly hunting groups scattered throughout the State who in fact were small militias. Unless you were a native to the area, the existence and activities of these militias were unknown.

According to the findings and determinations of Group X, Oregon was placed on a list identified as "undesirable for secession". The cons far outweighed the pros.

The Group began to evaluate the State of California. For the most part, they knew the outcome. However, they were obliged to follow the plan and to develop the pros and cons for determining if California would be a candidate for secession, A review of census data, voting records, and most recent polls taken by the Federal Government, State Agencies, and private organizations, including the CCP, proved very revealing. The most recent census data indicated that the State had a population in excess of thirty-two million citizens. The composition of the population was the most diverse in the nation. This was due to the influx of native born Americans into the State in the last fifty years. The mobility of the Americans could not be any better demonstrated than depicted by the Census Bureau during the last seven census'. The census data reflected roughly forty percent of the current population were born in the Midwest and eastern parts of the country.

This migration of Americans into the State was accompanied by the immigration of tens of thousands of people from Central and South America and the Far East, namely China, Japan, Korea, and Malaysia. This influx also included Europeans. All of these immigrants brought their own religions, customs, and traditions. The State's population truly represented every major race, religion, and culture on earth. Ironically, the African-Americans were a minority group in California. The Hispanics and Latinos were in the majority. The population was extremely diversified. This led to a very liberal political climate. Accommodations were necessary for coexistence. Clashes between races became more frequent.

California had the reputation for being very liberal dating back to the middle and late 20th Century. The dress codes, music, and life styles were already notoriously known as being free of any restraints. Hollywood obviously had an impact on the natives as well as on the nation. The drug culture was very pronounced in the State. This was due primarily to its proximity to Central and South America, the main avenues for drugs flowing into the country. The unusual long Pacific Ocean coast line also facilitated drugs coming into the country from the Far East without too much of a problem. Remote sites along the coast were used by drug dealers for importing drugs from the Far East. It was impossible for the State and Federal agents to check, let alone stop.

The State's education system was one of the best in the nation. The colleges and universities provided low cost, high quality educations. Especially noteworthy were the research facilities in medicine. Students from all parts of the globe were attracted to California schools. The liberal reputation of the environment did not detract prospective foreign students from attending the schools.

Data available to Group X relatively to elections was very interesting. Less than fifty percent of the population eligible to vote were registered voters. Of the eligible voters, only forty percent bothered to vote in the last two national elections. These were unbelievably low figures. Apparently the population of California was not interested in who was running the State or the nation. This was an interesting statistic. With that type of apathy, the State could be easily taken over by radical elements.

The sea ports of San Francisco and San Diego were outstanding. The access to the outside world was also enhanced by the numerous smaller ports and major air terminals. The long coast line and boundary of the State with neighboring Nevada were both considered disadvantages. These would be difficult to patrol. This was already proven in the State's war on drugs and illegal immigrants.

The State's border with Mexico was considered a detriment. The border was impossible to control against illegal immigrants and drugs. Both caused major problems not only in the State but throughout the nation. The illegal immigrants came not only from Mexico and Central and South America but as far away as China. The drugs were coming primarily from Central and South America. The entire border was like a sieve.

The State's economy was very sound. The major industries of farming, electronics, defense, fishing, tourism, and manufacturing provided ample employment for thousands.

The size of the State, its large population, the defense industries, and its relatively high representation in Congress (due to its population) were detriments to secession from the Group's point of view. Of greater concern were the liberal policies of the State. No restrictions on immigration. Unrestricted sexual partnerships. Free and open life styles that were contrary to sound Christian ideals. It did not take Group X long to identify the State as "undesirable for secession". They did not believe that it was too early to do so.

The Group decided to take a one day break to evaluate their schedule, status to date, and to rest. They did take a short walk into the woods to clear their minds and refresh their bodies. This respite would prepare them for the long stretch ahead. It would be their only break in the proceedings.

Group X addressed the map of the United States, specifically the East and Golf coasts. The question was one of approach. After some deliberation the Group agreed unanimously that they would begin the next phase of analyzing which State should be targeted for secession from the United States starting with Maine and proceeding down the coast line to Texas.

The same procedure would be followed that they applied to the west coast. Each State would be addressed. After analysis, the State would be labeled as undesirable or acceptable for consideration. The final selection would be determined after the total review was be completed. Based on their findings and conclusion, they would submit their recommendation to the head of the CCP. Their rationale would accompany their final report. It was time to return to the work at hand.

The weather in Idaho was normal for October. The cold air was moving into the area rapidly. Snow began to fall ever so lightly. The environment was conducive to working indoors.

The State of Maine was the subject. All of the materials and statistical data were placed on the table. The first item addressed was the population of the state. Although the State was the largest in terms of land area in New England, only approximately 3.2 million inhabitants were recorded on the last official census in the year 2020. This was considered very favorable by the Group. The relatively low population would make the task of taking control of the internal elections much easier. In this respect, it was considered ideal.

The population was comprised primarily of 4th and 5th generation native born Americans. The number of immigrants into the State since the turn of the century was one of the lowest in the nation. Maine was not known for having great employment opportunities. Its climate was not considered friendly to immigrants from the Far East and Central and South America. The summers were acceptable but the winters were considered too harsh. The majority of the citizens were Christians. There were no other significant religious groups in the State.

The State had few industries. The principal employment was in fishing and occupations associated with its vast forests and wood resources. Some light manufacturing was located in the western part of the State. The service industry played a significant role in providing low paying jobs.

The State had received devastating blows to its economy in the later part of the 20th Century. There were relatively few farms. The land was not conducive to farming. There were many abandoned farms throughout the State. It lost its textile and clothing industries to overseas areas. The global economy had an impact on the State from which it did not recover. This was an item of special note to the Group.

On the positive side of the ledger, the State education system was one of the best in the nation. There was no nonsense permitted in the schools. Maine was considered conservative in all respects. Politically it voted CCP in the last ten State and national elections.

Maine led the nation in the year 2020 in the percent of eligible voters who registered to vote, i.e., seventy percent. It also recorded the highest percent of registered voters who voted in the state and national elections that same year, i.e., sixty-five percent. Voter apathy was unknown in the State.

The State's coast line, exceeding 200 miles, its sea and air ports were ideal. These provided ample access to the outside world. The State had borders with Quebec and New Brunswick, Canada. These could be considered good neighbors. Quebec had attempted to separate from Canada in recent years. They could be considered as sympathetic to the CCP cause. Maine was also bordered by New Hampshire. A State that voted Republican in the last state and national elections. The State had the reputation of being close to the extreme right wing of the Party. Maine's border with New Hampshire was extensive. It was also close to the States of Massachusetts, Vermont, and Rhode Island. The last two States could be considered in the CCP camp.

The Group had no difficulty in adding Maine to a list of candidates for secession from the United States. In fact, it was the first eastern State identified as such by the Group.

Massachusetts was reviewed with some bias. The State had a reputation for being very liberal. It voted solidly Democratic in the past several State and national elections. There was some support for the CCP. Its population numbered in excess of six million in the 2020 census. The State had excellent sea and air ports that would be more than adequate to satisfy the Group. A review of the voting records indicated voter apathy. The number of eligible voters to register and subsequently to vote were below the fiftieth percentile in both categories. It was a mixed picture.

Economically the State was in excellent condition. Unemployment was below 5 percent. The State was blessed with a diversified industrial base. The exodus of textile and shoe industries overseas in the late 20th century was replaced with an influx of high technology companies.

The geographical location of the State was reviewed by the Group. It had excellent sea and air terminals. Its schools, road networks, and public utilities were considered to be above average. There were no known organized militias in the State. However, its reputation for liberal policies was well documented and considered a major problem by the Group.

After due deliberation, Group X decided to consider Massachusetts as an undesirable candidate for secession. The negative aspects outweighed the favorable factors.

New Hamshire was analyzed due to its access to the Atlantic Ocean. This was consistent with satisfying the sea port criteria. Its air terminals had potential for developing them to accommodate overseas flights.

Its border with Canada, primarily the Province of Quebec, was considered a plus factor. Again, this was due to the history of the Province. The sea port capabilities were considered too limited. It would not accommodate the free flow of shipping in and out of the State if it would secede from the United States.

The coastline was too short. A blockade could be too easily enforced.

The State had a relatively sound economy. Its consisted of agriculture, forestry and fishing, mining (granite) and light manufacturing. In addition, transportation and communications played a vital role in its business activities. Its commerce was diversified.

The Group determined that the State did have a serious problem related to its geography. It was bordered by Canada on the north, the Atlantic on the south, Vermont on the west, Massachusetts on the south-west, and Maine on the East. If New Hamshire would be selected for secession, it would physically cut-off Maine from the rest of the United States. Group X determined that the nation would never permit this to happen. They were correct in this conclusion.

The Group eliminated New Hampshire from consideration. It was added to the list of undesirable States for targeting.

Group X decided to consider Rhode Island, Connecticut, and Delaware as a group. Obviously the States were too small to facilitate future significant increases in population. True, they had pro-CCP voters, access to the sea, but they were also small in area. Too small for consideration. There was also the problem of having high profiles. It would be more difficult to infiltrate the States with CCP backers.

The States had limited sea and air port facilities. Their economic conditions were good. Unemployment was less than 5 percent in each of the States.

Each of the three States had low voter turn-out in the last three State and national elections. This suggested that each of the States would be easy targets to control with a good organizational plan. However, the size of the States and their proximity to liberal neighbors made the decision by the Group to consider them undesirable relatively easy.

The State of New York would consume several days of the Group's time. There were many variables to consider. The size of the state, its population in terms of numbers, the economy, and geographical location were evaluated in detail.

The State had the reputation of being indecisive. The political status changed with almost each election. It wavered between being Republican and Democrat. The voters were unpredictable. This was vividly clear in past elections and the low voter registrations and participation in elections. Less than 45 percent of the eligible voters bothered to register. Barely 50 percent of the registered voters went to the polls in the State and national elections in the year 2020.

The state's population represented every ethnic background, race, and religion on the face of the earth. The city of New York was like a bee hive. People were coming and going at a pace that was unequalled in any other part of the country. There appeared to be no stability to the population. There was some stability in the central and northern parts of the State.

Immigration was heavy. Legal and illegal aliens were saturating the city of New York. The aliens were lost in the maze of the inner city. No one could identify the true numbers of illegal aliens in the State. Some were employed in the central part of the State working on farms. Thousands were employed in the various service industries throughout the State.

The economy of the state supported every one who wanted to work. Its unemployment was less than 4 percent. The state's economy included farming, light and heavy industries, high technology, international commerce, tremendous tourism, financial activities, transportation, and a long list of various diverse businesses.

Its seaport facilities were the best on the east coast. Its air terminals were the envy of all other States. It was amazing that with all of the chaotic conditions in the State, it still managed to operate effectively.

Group X reviewed the geographic location of the State. The State bisected the entire eastern States from the United States, from the Atlantic Ocean to the Canadian border. This was extremely significant.

The Group had no doubt that this feature coupled with the history of voting would be major factors to drop the State from contention. Other aspects including the mass immigrations and liberal views on abortion, sexual preferences, and similar controversial attitudes reaffirmed the Group's decision to consider the State undesirable for secession.

New Jersey was studied with great interest. The State's voting history was CCP and Republican. This immediately drew the attention of the Group.

The census of 2020 revealed several interesting factors. The State had a population of eight million plus. Statistics indicated that the majority of inhabitants were 4th and 5th generation natives of the State. The State had the reputation of being strongly opposed to immigration and abortion. It favored strong penalties for major crimes. The State had close ties with the CCP.

The economy of the State was diversified. It included high technology, farming, light industries, and was the headquarters for many major corporations. One of it largest industries centered around Atlantic City and the gambling casinos. Of course this was one feature that the CCP opposed, at least on the surface. But, again, the CCP accommodated some strange bed-fellows.

One very salient feature of the voting records was the revelation of voter apathy. Less than fifty percent of the eligible voters registered to vote. This was accompanied by the records that only 35 percent of the registered voters went to the polls in the 2020 election. That was bad news on one hand. However, it was good news for the Group. It suggested that the State could be easily controlled at elections. New Jersey was added to the list of contenders.

Moving down the eastern seaboard, the Group addressed the State of Maryland.

Maryland had voted Democratic in the last three state and national elections. This was a bad omen. On the other hand, the voters had the reputation of being strongly in support of the CCP principals. This was particularly true of the pro-life issue. The State also supported the gun lobby.

The 2020 census reflected a population of slightly over five million people. Most of these were 4th and 5th generation Americans. The number of immigrants since the turn of the century was less than one hundred thousand. The State did have a mixture of ethnic, racial, and religious groups.

The economy of the State was good. An unemployment factor of less than six percent staled steady for several years. Farming, diverse light industries, tourism, and fishing were the main industries. The port operations of Baltimore continued to grow. The location of the port was viewed by the Group as a major problem. It was inland, at the far end of the Chesapeake Bay. Practically a suburb of the nation's capital, Washington, D.C. There was no further discussion.

Maryland was considered undesirable for secession.

The State of Virginia was next on the list of the Group. The first observation made was the proximity of Virginia to the nation's capital. It was bordered by the Potomac River, North Carolina, West Virginia, and Washington, D.C.

Other than being adjacent to the nation's capital, Virginia's neighbors to the west were ideal. West Virginia, with its armed militias, was considered friendly to the CCP. The same was true for North Carolina. Historically, these two states were Democratic strongholds prior to World War II. They joined the Republican camp in the later part of the 20th century.

Virginia's access to the outside world via sea and air were excellent. There were some obvious problems. Its major air port was located near D.C. There were other air terminals in the State but none equalled Dulles Airport.

The state's population neared seven million. Voter turnout was average. About forty percent of the registered voters bothered to vote in the national elections. Unfortunately, this was indicative of the national voter apathy.

Group X did not deliberate long in concluding that Virginia would be added to the list of undesirables. They recognized that the State voted Republican and had radical right wing supporters of the CCP. But the State's proximity to the nation's capital could not be overlooked. It was believed that the strength in the State could be used effectively in supporting the CCP in its ultimate objectives.

North Carolina was the next State to be considered. The past voting history made it a likely candidate for secession. The recent national elections reflected the strong ties to the Republican Party and the CCP. North Carolina, as so many States in the South, was traditionally Democratic until the later part of the 20th Century. Since that time, it constantly voted Republican and, since the establishment of the Christian Coalition Party, CCP, Several factors influenced the change.

North Carolina voters were strong supporters of pro-life. Many clung to the ideas of State's rights. The voters were not enamored with the policies of the Democratic Party. In particular they were not in support of the immigration policies and the anti-gun movement. The post WW II integration movement in the country met with opposition throughout the South. North Carolina was no exception. An armed militia was known to exist in the State that was active politically.

The recent census reflected a significant growth in population. The State became the home of many high technology companies. This feature offset the loss of some industries to overseas locations. The census recorded a population of approximately 7.5 million citizens. By far the majority were born in the State. There were new immigrants but not in significant numbers. The reputation of the State, i.e., Republican and CCP but more meaningfully having radical right wing elements, did not go unnoticed by new arrivals to the United States. Information of this nature traveled rapidly to the new immigrants and various organizations, including churches, who sponsored new immigrants.

The voting record of the State was poor. Only forty five percent of the population eligible to vote were registered. Of the registered voters, less than thirty-five percent voted in the last two State and national elections. This identified the State as a potential "easy" target for secession.

With the influx of high tech firms into the State, the educations system was dramatically upgraded to satisfy the new demand. This was true particularly of the Universities and Colleges. The State gained the reputation for having outstanding training capabilities. This in turn attracted more businesses to the State, including foreign companies. The State was ready to accept any business that would improve employment opportunities for its citizens.

The Group determined that the State lacked good sea port facilities. Access to the Atlantic Ocean was limited in this respect. This was somewhat offset by the more than adequate air terminals located throughout the State.

An advantage recognized by the Group were the neighboring States. All were considered CCP friendly. The Group decided that the size of the population was too high to control in elections. A second significant feature was the lack of adequate sea port facilities. It was considered that North Carolina could be used to support the goals of the CCP by remaining a part of the United States.

South Carolina had a population of almost four million citizens in the 2020 census. Ninety percent could trace their roots five generations back as residents of the State. There was no doubt that the State was pro-CCP. As other southern States, it too became a Republican stronghold following the post WW II years. It had a strong reputation for being anti-integration and immigration as recently as the 1980's. It began to case its stance on both issues to comply with the new laws on integration and with the growing world economy.

Similar to many other southern States, South Carolina took the initiative to attract foreign companies to locate businesses in the State. Taxes and other benefits were used to lure foreign industries. They were very successful in their efforts.

The State did have the same problem with getting its citizens to vote as did most States. Less than forty-five percent of eligible citizens bothered to register. Of the registered voters, only forty percent voted in the 2020 election. At this point, Group X concluded that voter apathy in the United States was universal. They also recognized that this favored their cause. It was much easier to win elections throughout the land. They did not lose sight of this fact. It would come into play in reaching their ultimate goal.

The State did have good sea and air facilities. These features were mandatory far consideration of secession. South Carolina was part of a block of southern States that were considered solidly behind the pro-life and CCP movement. However, the Group believed that the State could be counted upon to support the CCP ideals under any circumstances. The State did have radical right wing elements, including an armed militia, very active in the political process.

The Group was divided on whether to consider the State for secession. The three members of the Group who were themselves extreme right wing, favored a yes vote. The other three members voted negative. The rational of the voters to not consider South Carolina as a target was primarily due to the wide spread knowledge of the activities of the militia. The radical members of the Group acquiesced. They did not want to unduly alert the others to their own secret agenda.

The Group placed South Carolina on the undesirable list.

The Group next reviewed its data on the State of Georgia. As in all other States, the first items considered were the recent census and voting records.

According to the 2020 census, the State had a population of roughly 7.4 million. As in the case of Georgia and other States in the South, most of the residents were 4th and 5th generation natives.

The State was considered solidly belonging to the CCP. Its history in this respect also compared to its neighboring States. It favored the CCP causes, such as, pro-life, anti-immigration and gun control, less Federal interference with State's rights, and fewer Federal regulations.

A review of the 2020 election data indicated only forty-five percent of the State's eligible voters registered to vote.

Less than thirty-five per cent of those bothered to vote.

Certainly a dismal picture. This was consistent with some of the neighboring States. It was no wonder that it took little effort of organized political factions to take control of the local, State, and national elections. It was an American tragedy.

The State did have radical right wing supporters who broke away from the Republican Party. Their abandonment of the Republican Party was due to the Party leaders' wavering support of the pro-life movement and other right wing causes. The State had a strong militia that was very active in the political arena.

The group was impressed with the port facilities in Georgia. Although limited in numbers, this was offset by the quality. The air terminals were determined to be acceptable. As part of the "solid southern block", the Group believed that the State could be very supportive of the ultimate CCP goals. However, they decided to not include the State as a target for secession. They believed that State could fit the needs of the CCP in a supportive role.

Florida was the next State to be reviewed. The Group found the data on the State very interesting. A population in excess of fourteen million plus was recorded in the 2020 census. This figure in itself was considered a negative. However, after viewing the voting records, the Group reconsidered its initial observation.

The census indicated that the majority of the population were relatively recent arrivals. Most were retirees. Very few were native born Floridians. This coupled with the voting records suggested that there would be little, if any, problem in controlling the elections in the State by any political party. Of the eligible voters, only forty percent were registered. Less than thirty percent of the registered voters bothered to vote. The data reflected the attitude of the population. Most considered themselves temporary residents. Many came to live in the State to spend their last years.

The economy was very good. The State thrived through its senior citizens, tourists, space industry, and high technology firms that were attracted due to the climate.

The sea and air terminals were ideal. The coast line on the Gulf and Atlantic Ocean were perfect, Foreign trade could be developed to the advantage of the State. The State could be self supporting. It had an abundance of farms, including dairy farms. Its bordering States were CCP controlled. The State itself was divided politically. No political Party could lay claim to dominance. The CCP did have a good base. There were no known radical right wing groups. The State had a large population of minorities, primarily African-American and Cuban-American.

With all of the aspects analyzed and digested, the Group decided that Florida would be added to the list of undesirables. The rationale was that the State was too large, unreliable politically, and too diverse racially and ethnically.

Alabama proved to be a State that would not require too much time to analyze. It was considered solid CCP politically. It did have elements of the extreme right wing. It had an armed militia that was interconnected with other militias in the United States. It still harbored strong discrimination and anti-immigration practices. The Republican Party had the second largest political backing in the State. There was no question that from a political point of view, the State would be a good candidate for secession. However, there were some disadvantages.

In Mobile, the State had good access to the sea. But, the coast line was short and could be easily blocked. The State's airports were more than adequate. The global economy proved to be a bonanza for the State. It attracted several foreign firm by providing tax incentives for establishing activities in the State.

There were three significant problems. The reputation of the State for its discrimination practices was a major factor. Of significance to the Group were the low education standards in the State and the low voter turnouts. The 2020 census recorded 4.3 million residents. Of the total number of eligible voters in the State, less than fifty percent registered. Of these, less than thirty percent voted in the last two national elections.

Alabama was considered a good supporting State. It was added to the list of undesirable States for secession.

Louisiana was almost a duplicate of Alabama. It was similar to Alabama in many respects. The population was about the same, Its education system, although slightly better, was considered by national standards to have serious shortfalls.

Voter apathy was not as significant as in Alabama. But, it was nothing outstanding. It fared slightly better than other southern States.

Its economy was considered weak. Fishing, agriculture, light manufacturing, transportation and communications, plus some high technology boosted the State's commerce. New Orleans and its port operations added substantially to the economy.

The CCP was the main political force in the State. The State was considered very conservative. It aligned itself with the pro-life cause. However, it also had a strong anti-immigration and gun control lobby. A militia was know to exist in the State.

Group X viewed the State as one that could depended upon to support its ultimate goal. The State was added to the list of undesirables.

Texas was the last of the candidate States to be reviewed. The Group had thus far identified only two States as candidates for secession from the United States. The States of Washington and Maine were in a category by themselves.

Texas had a population of 19.3 million citizens in the 2020 census. Of these, roughly sixty percent were eligible to vote. Of the eligible voters, seventy percent were registered In the 2024 elections, less than thirty eight per cent of the registered voters bothered to exercise their right.

The major part of the population was comprised of Latinos and Hispanics. This was anticipated as early as the turn of the century. The migration, legal and illegal, of these groups from Mexico, Central and South America increased dramatically beginning in the 1970's. This migration was attributed to several factors. The desire to escape from poverty and the poor economic conditions in those nations was a major factor. A second ingredient was the corrupt political governments that drained their economies. The average citizen had no leverage. Those who did manage to get to the United States in the early years, communicated the advantages and job opportunities available in the country to their relatives and friends. Everyone wanted to share in the good life.

These immigrants were hard working. But, their history of not trusting politicians resulted in very low voter turnouts. Who could blame them. However, this voter apathy could be taken advantage of by any well organized political party. This was duly noted by the Group.

Texas always did have excellent sea and air facilities. Houston, Galveston/Texas City, and Port Arthur had excellent port accommodations, Dallas/Ft. Worth, Austin, and Houston were internationally know for their excellent air terminals.

The State had a variety of commercial activities, Fishing, Agriculture, mining, transportation, light and heavy manufacturing, tourism, forestry, and, of course, the cattle industry. There was no shortage of commerce. This was, in fact, the reason for the mass immigration of Latinos and Hispanics into the State. Texas always had a labor shortage. Being in proximity to Mexico and Central and South America was ideal.

The education system did have a few problems. This was due primarily at the elementary level. The language barrier was at the root of the difficulties encountered by the immigrants in the State. Their desire to better themselves and outstanding drive to be educated was generally overcome by the time the students reached the secondary level of education.

The State Universities were equal to any in the nation. Each had more applications for attendance than they could accept.

The student bodies represented every culture, religion, race, and ethnic group in the nation. Foreign students from Europe, Asia, and the Middle east were represented at almost every University and College in the State.

A key factor that came out of the review of the past two national elections, in addition to the low voter turnout, was the preponderance of the CCP vote. A further review indicated that militias and the extreme right wing of the Republican Party were the reasons.

The Democrats were the second largest block of voters. The Social Scientist Party (SSP) came in a distant third. As in other States, the Freedom Party (FP) and their environmental platform came in a last. They were truly the smallest Party.

The lack of a significant SSP vote was surprising to the Group. After all, the SSP was dominated by the Latinos and Hispanics on the ticket. The history and mentality of this group of people was difficult to overcome.

Group X considered all of the pros and cons in considering the State as a target for secession. Of all of the States reviewed, Texas provided the biggest challenge to the Group.

Its population of over nineteen million, the voting records, the composition of its citizens, the commercial aspects, the CCP recent victories in the State, and its neighboring States were all reviewed repeatedly. In the final analysis, the Group made a decision. However, it was not unanimous. This was the only State where the vote was not unanimous.

Group X decided to add the State of Texas to Washington, Maine, and New Jersey as potential targets for secession from the United States. A special note was added to indicate that the nomination of Texas was not unanimous. The three radical right wing members were able to gain the support of one other of the six person Group to vote in favor of accepting Texas.

On January 1, 2026, Group X submitted their report and recommendations to the Head of the CCP. Their task was completed on schedule.

CHAPTER 6

THE DECISION AND STRATEGY FOR SECESSION

At the beginning of January, 2026, Group X presented the report to the President of the Christian Coalition Party and his two executive Vice-Presidents at a meeting in Charlottesville, Virginia. The meeting took place at a horse farm near the campus of the University of Virginia. The site and location were carefully chosen in order not to attract any undue attention. The horse fare was owned by a strong supporter of the Christian Coalition Party and a personal friend of the Head of the CCP. The house was screened for eavesdropping devices to assure complete privacy and security. This was done by the owner based on the request of the head of the CCP.

Comparable to the facilities and arrangements for Group X in Idaho, similar provisioning of supplies was undertaken to facilitate the three key players staying in seclusion for the anticipated thirty days that were set aside for their decision making process. The owner of the farm did provide the team with his personal house-keeping staff, including a chef and servant. These were proven faithful employees who had served the farm for the past thirty plus years.

The schedule called for Group X to stay at the farm for three days in order to brief the decision team. After the briefing and answering questions posed by the team, Group X would depart after being sworn to secrecy and the three CCP leaders would begin their final decision process. This would include developing a strategy to culminate the action. The steps to be taken would be delineated and the necessary follow-up would also be scheduled. A key factor to be addressed would be a fall-back position for the CCP if, for whatever reason, the planned secession would falter. The CCP did not want to be viewed as the major player in the action.

Group X spent the better part of three days briefing the party of three on the entire report. They made every effort to explain their methodology, the thought processes, and the rationale that went into their review of the United States to determine which States would be candidates for secession. Special emphasis was presented on the reasons for dropping any of the States from the target action. This seemed the easiest avenue for presenting their conclusions relative to the States that would survive their review and make the list of candidate States.

Group X presented their rationale for deleting States almost in the same sequence that they followed in their own deliberations in Idaho.

Their rationale for dropping Alaska and Hawaii from consideration was first on the agenda. The Head of the CCP and his two Vice-Presidents did not have any questions. They reasoned that the logic of Group X was valid. The fact that Hawaii voted Democratic in the last several national elections was certainly very meaningful. In regards to Alaska, the three members also concurred that the State, although viewed as strong CCP and supported by the Republican Party, had too high a profile. They realized that the people of the United States would not be anxious to lose the State. It was too important to the nation from an economic point of view. It was rich in natural resources, including oil.

Group X then addressed the land-locked States that were dropped from consideration for secession. The need for access to the outside world was a paramount consideration. It would be stupid for the CCP to target a State that would be surrounded by hostile forces. The team recognized that the State selected must be capable of having political and commercial activities with other nations of the world. This would be necessary for survival. The worst scenario for a State seeking secession would be to isolate itself from the outside world. From a practical point of view, the group believed that selecting a land-locked State for secession would doom the planned action to failure. The three CCP executives agreed totally with the conclusions of Group X.

The decision to not consider favorably any of the States bordering the Great Lakes was also endorsed by the CCP leaders. The confines provided by the St. Lawrence Seaway were totally unacceptable. This factor coupled with any of the States that shared borders with Canada, with the exception of Maine, were more than adequate reasons to concur with the findings and recommendations of Group X.

Prior to Group X addressing the candidate States for secession, they provided several salient observations they made during the study. First and foremost, they commented on the universal voter apathy in all of the United States. Statistically, an average of only 45 percent of eligible voters were registered. Of the number of voters who were registered, an average of 35 percent voted in the last two national elections. This was considered a national disgrace.

Another factor that Group X considered significant, was the large number of immigrants to the United States. This phenomena started in the 20th century, around the year 1965. There was no special reason associated with this activity and time period. An accompanying oddity was the observation that the immigrants came from all corners of the globe. However, the greatest number came from Central and South America. The immigrants from Mexico dominated the field. This was due to many reasons. A corrupt Mexican government was on top of the list. Many citizens of Mexico came to the United States looking for a better life. They had no difficulty crossing the border to a more stable and lucrative life-style.

The second highest number of immigrants came from the Far East, Koreans, Chinese, and Malaysians domineered the vast numbers of new arrivals from that region. There were also sizeable numbers of immigrants from Vietnam. Economics was the main driving force. The United States had the reputation of being a land of opportunity. They wanted a share of the pie. Ironically, the nation's business leaders, ranchers and farmers pressed the politicians in Washington, D.C., to permit more migrant workers and immigration into the country.

The economy of the country was expanding. Labor shortages were apparent throughout the land. The United States was experiencing the same labor problems encountered by Germany in the post World War II years when that nation recruited labor from Italy, Turkey, Spain, and Poland to meet the demands of the country's flourishing economy. And, like Germany, employers from the United States recruited people from the four corners of the globe to satisfy the demands for labor. Not all Americans were happy with this turn of events. The extreme right wing, including the militias, opposed the mass immigrations. Controlling inflation by this method would prove costly to many politicians.

European immigrants were a distant third. This was contrary to the numbers from central Europe who emigrated to the United States in the tens of thousands during the 19th and 20th centuries. The National Archives had records documenting daily arrivals of passenger ships from Europe with hundreds of new immigrants. The European Union provided peace and good economic conditions in the post WW II years. These were powerful factors in curtailing mass emigrations. A second factor was the much publicized crime factor in the United States and the relatively poor public education system.

Group X had a good grasp of the causes of the tremendous influx of legal and illegal immigrants. They surmised that the global economy operating at the time, caused a labor shortage in the United States. Goods and services from the United States were sought by countries throughout the world. The nation could not satisfy the consumer demands without opening the door to mass immigration. Without this outside help, the nation's industries and farms could not survive.

Group X also noticed a shift in demographics of the nation's population. The 2010 and 2020 census' reflected a major shift of the country's population from the northern and eastern States to the west and south-western States. Also, the mid-atlantic States had shown slight increases in population.

Of greater significance, the census data also reflected the dramatic increase in Hispanics and Latinos in the nation's population. They were the largest racial and ethnic minority group in the country according to the 2020 census. This was a surprise to everyone. Based on earlier studies, It was believed that this would not occur until the year 2050.

African-Americans were a distant second according to the census data. This was expected to occur later in the century.

Based on voter data available from the Census Bureau, the various political parties, private sources, and local and state voter registration records, Group X concluded that the CCP had the largest number of members. The Republican Party was a distant third. This was due to the number of Republican voters who switched to the CCP. The Democratic Party, due to its pro-choice stance, lost many followers. However, it was able to place second in respect to numbers voting Democratic.

The Social Scientist Party (SSP) was a distant fourth while the Freedom Party (FP), primarily environmentalists and animal rights advocates, was the fifth largest political party in the United States.

The CCP executives decided to take a few hours to digest the material they covered prior to proceeding with the final report of Group X. Having done so, they were eagerly waiting for Group X to complete their report.

With this background, Group X proceeded to address the four candidate States they were recommending to the CCP for secession from the United States. Washington, Maine, New Jersey, and Texas would be presented in that order, The Group would also submit its recommendation to the three executives. This would complete their assignment.

Each of the six members of Group X participated in making the presentations. The Group indicated their rationale for selecting the State of Washington as a target for secession. Its outstanding sea and air terminals provided ideal facilities for access to the world. The neighboring State of Idaho had strong leanings for the CCP ideals. The major portion of the population was in favor of the pro-life movement. Idaho elected CCP candidates to State and national offices. The State also had a solid Republican vote, one that supported the CCP candidates across the board. Idaho also had a very strong and active militia. It was considered an extreme right wing organization.

The negatives included the State's boundaries with Canada and with the State of Oregon. In the former case, there was no doubt that Canada would not be sympathetic with any State attempting to secede from the United States. Oregon voted Democratic in the last two national elections.

The armed militia located in Idaho could also be considered a negative. Although the CCP sought their support because of the mutual stance on pro-life, the CCP did not want to openly endorse a militant group.

After answering several questions from the three CCP executives, Group X proceeded to present its report on the State of Maine.

There were many advantages to targeting Maine as the State to be selected for secession. Its diversity of industries, good air and sea terminals that would provide global access, and its relatively small population of slightly over one million were cited as advantages. Maine was definitely in the CCP camp. The population took voting seriously as evidenced by the last several elections. It was strong pro-life. Maine had one of the lowest abortion rates in the entire nation,

The neighboring States were strong supporters of the CCP. The second largest political Party in the neighboring States was the Republican Party. The Freedom Party had some support but not significant. Even the two neighboring Canadian Provinces of Quebec and New Brunswick were considered friendly.

Quebec's attempt to secede from Canada in the late 20th century placed it in the "sympathetic camp". Having neighbors that would be supportive to their cause was considered a firm requirement. It would be more than just desirable to have buffers between itself and the remainder of the nation. Strategically it would be mandatory especially if the President of the United States would be forced politically to attempt to prevent the secession.

The geographical location of the State was considered an asset to secession. It was somewhat isolated, located in the upper northeastern part of New England. Perhaps it was this factor that discouraged immigrants from settling in Maine.

The negative aspects were few and not significant. Its proximity to Canada was offset by the friendly Provinces. Its population was relatively small. The economy was sound. There was some skepticism if the natives would be willing to give up this good life for something unknown.

The CCP executives were very impressed with the data presented by Group X. There were no questions from the CCP group.

New Jersey was presented by the Group with less enthusiasm than the State of Maine, Yes, they did consider New Jersey as a likely candidate for secession. It had strong CCP and Republican leanings. It had a history of favoring the issues associated with the right wing. Voter registration and turn-out was high considering the national averages. It was not invaded by immigrants as were some states in the East. It had a sound economy, diversified and lucrative. The unemployment factor hovered around 5 percent. It did have very good sea and air terminals.

The education system was one of the best along the east coast. The state was known for being pro-life. There were some disadvantages, however.

Its proximity to the nation's capital and New York were considered major deterrents. The crime rate was comparatively high for the size of the population. There was no special reason for this situation. The State had a high profile in Washington, D.C. due to several factors, primarily its political strength in the Senate. Hence, the Group did not recommend it for selection. The Groups recommendation was consistent with its decisions in other instances where it did not want to nominate a State that would raise too many questions in Washington.

Texas was presented as the third and final candidate for secession by Group X.

The strong points in favor of Texas were many. Its CCP and Republican Party records were a given, Texas had voted along CCP and Republican ideals in the last three state and national elections. The State was strong pro-life. Its education system was one of the best in the nation. The State had a very diversified business base. Its air and sea ports were among the best in the country. The State had a reputation for having very strong right wing elements.

The population of Texas in the 2020 census was in excess of nineteen million citizens. The population was still growing. There was no end in sight. This was due in part to the migration of people from the Midwest and northeastern States. Of course, the biggest influx was due to the migration of Latinos and Hispanics from Central and South America to Texas. The later group consisted primarily of Catholics who were also strong supporters of the pro-life issue.

The neighboring States were considered friendly. However, there was some question if they would support the secession movement. This was somewhat hazy.

Group X proceeded to identify the possible negatives of selecting Texas as the target State. Serious consideration was given to the size of the State, both in terms of land area and population. It could be too large in both respects to digest. The make-up of the population was considered to be a threat to the success of secession. The recent migration of people from other parts of the country could cause serious problems to a secession movement. Of greater concern was the immigration of legal and illegal people from Central and South America. The voting records revealed the low voter participation. No doubt that this could also pose a major problem. This would be especially true in the national elections. Other political Parties, for example the Democratic Party, could seriously challenge the CCP for votes.

A salient point that was not lost on the Group was the key role Texas played in the past several Presidential elections. It was the pivot State. The nation followed the State of Texas in voting. Whichever way Texas voted, so went the nation. This was considered to be a critical item to the Group. They realized that the nation would react strongly if Texas would attempt to secede from the United States. Similar to New Jersey, its high profile was a serious detriment to secession from the United States.

Group X completed its presentation with one remaining action. After the CCP executives posed a few relevant questions to the Group on Texas, they asked Group X which of the four States they would recommend for secession.

Group X indicated that they held a secret ballot on this question amongst themselves prior to leaving their retreat in Idaho. Maine received six votes. The recommendation was unanimous. Group X was dismissed. Now it would be the decision of the CCP Group to make its choice.

The Head of the CCP and the two Vice-Presidents knew that they had an awesome task facing them. They did however relish their position. The first phase of the Party in reaching their goal was successfully completed. They were happy with the progress and the results thus far.

After the six members of Group X departed the farm, the head of the CCP and his two assistants decided to briefly review the findings and recommendations of Group X. They were very satisfied with the details presented by Group X and their rational on all aspects particularly relating to the States not considered for secession. The thought process that Group X pursued in identifying the three candidate States for secession was considered outstanding.

The leader of the Group suggested that they pursue their own decision process in selecting which of the three States to be targeted for secession. The next presidential elections would take place in the year 2028. Many actions would be scheduled to take place in order to have the plan in place and operational in time for these elections.

After three days of deliberation and reviewing their data on the States of Washington, Texas, New Jersey, and Maine, the decision was made to go with the State of Maine. All of the available information and the detailed briefing by Group X proved to be more than adequate to decide on Maine as the best target for secession from the United States. Now the challenge would be to develop the strategy to culminate the action and identify the steps to be taken to assure success of this daring and historical venture. The CCP would take advantage of their coalition involving the radical right wing elements, the many armed militias scattered throughout the country, and various Christian groups opposed to abortion.

The CCP leader and his two assistants spent the next several days discussing and planning the strategy to accomplish their objective. They recognized that the plan would have to be all encompassing, from the outset through the culmination including acceptance of the secession by the United States.

They began by analyzing the demographics of the all of the United States. The ethnic and racial make-up of each State was reviewed. This was data that Group X had recorded from the census of 2020. Based on voting records there was little if any doubt that the minority population generally voted Democratic. This was ironic in a sense. The minority groups had the largest families. Most were pro-life, Yet, as a rule, they voted for candidates on the Democratic ticket who were pro-choice. The obvious rationale was that the Democratic Party was strong on social and welfare issues.

A further review of the voting records identified the States that were definitely in the CCP camp. The same records also recorded the States that were strongly Democratic, the major opposition to the CCP.

By reviewing the census and voting information of all of the United States, it was determined that the CCP strategy would be to concentrate on influencing the state and national elections where the CCP was the major Party and on those states that were borderline. The latter would be states that did not have a dominant political Party Texas, Alabama, Louisiana, North and South Carolina, Georgia, Virginia, Indiana, Montana, Idaho, Alaska, and, of course, Maine were examples of States dominated by the CCP.

California, Florida, New York, Hawaii, and West Virginia were know to be heavily Democratic states.

Ohio, Illinois, Kentucky, Oregon, Colorado, and Iowa were examples of States whose past voting records suggested that they could be manipulated in different directions.

The team than reviewed the percentage of eligible voters who registered to vote in each state. Also, the number of registered voters who voted in the previous two national elections. Based on the findings of Group X, they knew that voter apathy prevailed in all of the states.

Based on these considerations, the CCP team determined that priority would be given in the forthcoming elections of 2028 in electing their candidates in the states that they dominated politically. Every measure would be taken to capture the local, state, and national offices. This would establish a sound foundation from which to launch their programs. It would also provide a base for assuring strong support of their ultimate objective involving the secession.

The team recognized the need for obtaining control of the borderline states, i.e., not solid in any political camp. It made sense to take advantage of the prevailing voter apathy in the states that were susceptible to political control. There was no doubt that a sizable amount of funds would be required for publicity and campaigning. The effort to raise funds for this effort would take various forms. But, there was no doubt that the necessary monies could be raised. The CCP had many benefactors. Businesses, individuals, various religious organizations, and, yes, foreign interests would be solicited.

The Party was dominated by people who had experience in raising funds for various religious and charitable causes.

The foreign interests were of some small concern, However, the group believed that this would be a lucrative source of monies for their cause. They were fully cognizant that there were certain countries that were hoping for the United States to weaken its international influence. In the mid 20th century, many political analysts had predicted that the United States would eventually destroy itself from within. There were foreign nations that had the same belief. They were certainly very happy and willing to assist the United States in this respect. Providing funding to the CCP for its ultimate objective was their pleasure. After all, it was in their interest to help the United States to destroy itself.

There were also some nations that believed they could profit from the plans of the CCP. It was no secret that the CCP was thinking of taking dramatic action involving secession. What was not publicly known was the extent the Party would go in this direction. The foreign nations that were willing to contribute financially to the CCP knew it was a gamble on their part, But, they believed that if the CCP was serious and did follow through with its action, there could be a big reward via trade relations with the new nation.

A special committee was established to raise funds for the CCP. This committee was located in Lynchburg, Virginia. The plan included organizing political fund raising efforts that would bring in the required monies into the national headquarters. All funds would be controlled by the CCP leadership at the national level. Funds would be distributed from Lynchburg. Total control would be extended over every dollar.

There were special prayer breakfasts scheduled in all of the major cities. Businesses and private citizens were invited by special invitation. The meetings were advertised in the local newspapers and on radio and television stations. This effort raised over one hundred million dollars in six months. The CCP leadership could not have been happier with the result. It was interesting that at many of these meetings, members of various state militias and extreme right wing groups were in attendance and in some instances even the principal speakers. The general public seemed unaware of the historic events unfolding. But, than again, it was typical of the American public.

The committee in charge of the fund raising used the U.S. mail to great advantage. Form letters were developed and designed to attract attention to the various causes of the CCP. The recipients were people who were know to favor the CCP including voters who made financial donations at one time or another to CCP candidates or causes. This was a national campaign. It was organized from the very top of the CCP to the precinct level. Every organizational level of the CCP was utilized in this effort.

The Party made maximum use of the high technology in communications. The Web site and internet were used to make contact with the tens of millions of U.S. citizens and foreign nationals. These solicitations also proved excellent for bringing in funds from all over the globe.

Of course there were the special interest groups, businesses, various institutions, religious and charitable organizations that were solicited. The responses were all very favorable.

With all of these efforts, the CCP had more than enough funds to wage a national political campaign.

The next step in the strategy was to assure that qualified and loyal CCP candidates would be chosen to run for the various elected offices throughout the land. This would be no easy task. The CCP organization would have to assure total organization from the head of the CCP down to the precinct and block captains. This would be the greatest challenge that the Party would face.

The leader of the CCP sent a form letter to each CCP state Party chairman directing that his letter be endorsed and forwarded to the next echelon reminding them of the necessity for the Party to have the best qualified candidates running for the various political offices in the State and at the local levels. Again, total control was advocated. The letter was well received. This action taken by the CCP leadership brought about the results desired.

Every elected position had a CCP candidate, either as an incumbent or a challenger, who was screened and approved for the office by the local and state political hierarchy.

The need for publicity for the Party's candidates was well recognized. All of the earlier successful efforts to raise funds for the elections would come into play. The local, state, and national newspapers, radio and television stations would carry the CCP's ideas, its agenda, and the endorsements of the candidates from the local to the national levels. The Party concentrated on the States that were known to be secured and on the borderline states. The least amount of campaign funds were directed to the states that were historically Democratic controlled. But even in those states, an effort was made to draw attention to the agenda of the CCP. This was a factor that the Party believed it could take advantage of in the planned secession effort. It wanted to make its agenda known to all Americans.

The publicity began in earnest in 2027 and continued until election eve in 2028. It was extremely successful. Every voter knew the CCP agenda and their candidates. It assured the Party of total control of the election.

Never in the history of the United States did a political party dominate an election as the CCP did in November, 2028. Every CCP office seeker was elected. There was no doubt that the very costly campaign publicity was successful. The combination of the Party's agenda, support of various religious groups who were pro-life, the armed militias, and, perhaps the most important ingredient, national voter apathy contributed to the victory of the CCP.

The voters in Maine elected a strong Governor, one who knew the ultimate objective of the Party. He was hand picked by the CCP leadership to run for the office to assure the success of the secession. It was critical that the highest elected official in the State be 100 % behind the planned action. This person, if the CCP plan for secession would prove to be successful, would be the leader of a new nation. Every effort was made to screen the candidate from the day he was born until his selection. His heritage, education, voting record, affiliations with various organizations, and political leanings were reviewed in extreme detail. There would be no room for error. The only fallacy in this procedure was that the leader of the CCP gave the total responsibility for selecting the candidate to his two executive vice-presidents.

The head of the CCP endorsed the selection without any further questions. This oversight would eventually prove to be a major blunder.

With the Presidential, Congressional, and State elections in November, 2028, the Christian Coalition Party had total control of the Presidency, Congress, and a majority of State Capitals. In addition, due to the expenditure of large sums of campaign monies, the CCP had influenced many Americans who voted along Party lines,

The CCP recognized that timing was crucial to assuring success of the final action in this drama. It would be wise for the Party to allow the State of Maine and the President and Congress to function in their respective elected positions for a short time. The plan provided for the Governor of Maine to announce the secession on January 1, 2029. This would allow the Governor to organize and implement operating procedures for the transition from a state to a nation. Many preliminary actions would be necessary, including identifying personnel appointments and provisions for raising revenues. It was mandatory that he surround himself with loyal aids.

Concurrently, the President of the United States and the Congressional members who were affiliated with the CCP would need to make plans on how to proceed with approval of the secession. In secret sessions, there was total agreement that the action would bring major protests from certain elements of the population and particularly from the other political parties. The strategy included coping with the objections without having to resort to use of the armed forces.

The mood of the nation was important to consider. The economy was flourishing. The unemployment rate was less than three percent. The majority of Americans owned their own homes. The immigration problem seemed to be under control even though illegal immigrants were still a problem in the eyes of the extreme right wing and militia groups. The pro-choice versus the pro-life factions were continuously at odds. But, as a whole, the nation was at peace and prospering.

The President of the United States and the CCP members of Congress met often to discuss the coming event. The Governor of Maine visited the White House and met with his compatriots in Congress and CCP Governors to discuss the forthcoming action and plans. It was through luck that none of the major news organizations gave too much notice to these meetings. It apparently did not seem news-worthy that the Governor of Maine was meeting so often with key elected officials throughout the country. On occasion, some news person would ask what the meetings covered. They were satisfied with the information that the spokesman gave, e.g., the meetings involved education or funding for highways. It was miraculous that the real reason for the meetings did not leak out.

On Thanksgiving Day, 2027, everything was in order. The President of the United States, the leader of the CCP and his two executive Vice-Presidents, and the Governor of Maine met at Camp David to solidify the secession of Maine. The date was established as January 1, 2028. The President of the United

States would place the military on alert to control any radical reactions even though none was expected. The Governor would make certain that his head of the National Guard would be prepared to control any protests in Maine to the announcement. The CCP Congressional leaders would be advised of the date and timing to facilitate their advising their constituents of the peaceful transition about to take place. The President would address the nation on January 2, 2028, of the approval and recognition of the new nation. He would indicate that since it was the will of the Maine voters, the country would honor their action. This would draw from several sources. The many years of scheming and planning by the CCP and the extreme right wing would finally produce rewards. Their ultimate objective to control the United States and its citizens would come to fruition. The remainder of the nation would be dumbfounded and would certainly look back at their indifference to the voting privilege that they squandered.

On January 1, 2028, the people of the United States would experience the most traumatic event in the country since the Civil War. The country would be in shock on hearing the announcement made on that date. The Governor of Maine, in a special message televised to the entire nation, declared that Maine was seceding from the United States and henceforth would be an independent nation. He stated Maine's sovereignty was the choice of its people and should be honored by the Government of the United States. The American people were traumatized. The reaction of the news media was foreseen. The nation was deluged with various news reports of corruption, collusion, treason, political sabotage, and other similar charges.

The evening of January 2, 2028, did nothing to ease the situation. The President of the United States addressed the nation as planned. His speech was conciliatory toward the action of the Maine Governor. A shock to the American people was his endorsement of the secession. This was totally unexpected. Chaos reigned in the newsrooms throughout the land. The American listeners and viewers were also amazed. The reaction from the Democratic and other political parties was slow in coming. They too were in shock about the developments of the last two days.

The CCP and the extreme right wing of both the CCP and Republican parties rejoiced on January 3, 2028. Their success was unimaginable. The American public was in shock. There was no violent reaction. The President of the United States was pleasantly surprised at this development. He cancelled the alert of the armed forces, everything seemed to be going unusually smoothly. Concurrently the Governor of Maine cancelled the call-up of the national guard.

The leadership of the Democratic, Social Scientist, and Freedom Parties were astounded by the developments. It took a few days for the impact to set in. The audacity of the Governor of Maine coupled with the President's public approval of the secession was considered treason. But, the die was cast and the action seemed to proceed without any radical reaction from the general population of the country.

The radical right wing of the CCP gloated over its successes. The time was near for them to exercise their own secret agenda. The timing was absolutely perfect. It was obvious that the American public was not going to cause a revolution over the secession. There were a few ugly incidents scattered throughout the land. But, there was no organized rebellion over the actions of the President or of the Governor of Maine. The leadership of the CCP was too enamoured with its successes to catch its breath and begin to organize its achievements. After all, they had control of the White House, the Congress of the United States, and a new nation under their sponsorship. What else could they ask for? They could afford to spend some time celebrating their victories. So they believed.

In the meantime, the Governor of Maine declared that the new nation would be named, "New America". He redesignated all of the offices as Federal offices. The National Guard became the official army of the New America. All of these events followed within thirty days of the secession from the United States. There were many actions still to be taken to reflect the new status of the country versus state. A plan was developed to make the total transition within sixty days. The entire objective was to establish an operating government as soon as possible, prior to any organized actions to disrupt the new regime.

In consideration of all of these various facets, the radical right wing decided to make its move. The Governor declared himself the President of the New America. What was formerly the state legislature was declared the Congress. Now was the time to act.

On February 1, 2028, the President of New America declared his nation's total independence. They were no longer associated with the Christian Coalition Party. Henceforth, all political parties would be banned from the new nation. The shock was felt throughout the world. The Head of the CCP knew that he was betrayed. He recognized that he was powerless to do or say anything. The past CCP actions to orchestrate the secession, its coordination with the various militias and the extreme right wing of the Republican Party, prevented the CCP from doing anything to change the course of events.

The Head of the CCP called a meeting of the main members and supposedly loyal supporters to review and discuss the developments. It was time to admit that they had been used by the extreme right wing and the militant militias. It was a difficult admission to make. The consequences of revealing their role could cause civil and violent disruptions throughout the land. They concluded that it was best to lay aside any open hostility toward the new nation and its leaders. The action would prove costly, nevertheless, in future elections. The CCP would no longer work in tandem with any other political Party to win an election. Losing the support of the militias and the extreme right wing would place the CCP in third position behind the Democratic and Republican Parties in that order.

In the meantime, the President of New America began to reach out to the bordering States for political support. This action was necessary to combat any unanticipated military move by the United States to negate the independence even though the action was closely coordinated months and years ago with the current President of the United States who was totally involved in the scheme from its inception. His stake was more political power. After all, his election was assured primarily to the support of the extreme elements that were now in control of the new nation. The campaign monies that came from foreign sources was due to the efforts of the extremists.

Days, weeks, and months passed without any major civil disorders either in the United States of within the new nation.

The leaders of the Democratic, Social Scientist, and Freedom Parties openly criticized the President of the United States for not taking any military action to negate the establishment of a new nation in the State formerly known as Maine. They too realized the potential internal conflict that could tear apart the heart of the country if the government lost control of the people,

The criticism of the CCP was constant for months. The President of the United States was somewhat relieved that the leaders of the opposing Parties did not direct their anger in his direction. As the months passed, the turmoil seemed to subside. This was anticipated by the CCP in its original estimates of the American public's reaction to its plan involving the secession. It was consistent with the findings of Group X and the voter apathy. The American Public seemed to be more concerned with its economic fortunes. They were more involved with the activities of the various professional sports activities than the political process that was ongoing in North America. The general public disregarded anything that did not directly impact their status in life.

The President of New America soon took actions that would reveal the new nation's policies and doctrines. He shocked not only the Americans but the world with his declarations. It was a wake up call for the United States. Even the CCP and Republican Party leaders were flabbergasted and speechless. The militias and extreme right wing of the Republican Party were overjoyed upon hearing the policies of the New America.

The city of Augusta, the capital of New America, would become the main attraction to the world's news media. Reporters from all over the globe would converge on Augusta to cover the unfolding of the dramatic events that were forthcoming.

CHAPTER 7

NEW AMERICA'S MODUS OPERANDI

The President of the New America had his own schedule of events that would transpire over the first several months of his tenure. He adopted policies that would shock not only the citizens of his new nation but the United States and foreign countries.

The President of the new nation consolidated his position by appointing known members of the militias and extreme right wing to key positions in his government. His Cabinet took the appearance of men and women who were known for having strong feelings on all of the issues of the extreme right wing. Ironically, he did not select any of his staff from the Christian Right. There was no question about the direction the President and the new nation were headed.

It took several months for events to unfold. In fact it was on September 1 that the true colors of New America would unfold. While the United States and the rest of the world were occupying themselves with economic problems related to the global markets, the President of New America decided to move boldly with his domestic and foreign policies in that order.

He scheduled a national television session at 7 P.M., September 1, 2028, to address his domestic policies. His office announced that the foreign policies of New America would be addressed on October 1. The President of New America crested a storm with his proclamations. Even the dedicated followers were amazed at the dramatic announcements that emanated from Augusta, the new nation's Capital. The unfolding events were similar to the era that dated back to the 1930's in Germany, Italy, and Japan.

After his initial opening comments that addressed the peaceful secession and establishment of New America, the President thanked the President and the people of the United States for accepting and recognizing the new nation. He also indicated his appreciation to the foreign governments who extended their congratulations to the new country. In separate messages, he extended his appreciation for the financial support that they provided to his government.

He proceeded to enunciate his domestic policies to the world.

The first issue involved pro-life. The Nation would not permit abortions for any reason. The performance of abortions would be considered a criminal act, subject to prison terms. Any medical personnel performing or involved in any way with the abortion act would lose their licenses to practise in the State and be subject to criminal prosecution. Putting it bluntly to the listening audience, abortions would be banned in the nation beginning immediately.

The President went on to explain his position and stated that the people of New America had indicated their support of this policy. There were many in the new nation who favored pro-choice. This pronouncement by the President immediately triggered a barrage of phone calls and telegrams to the President protesting the policy. And this was even prior to the remainder of his speech. One could not imagine a more divisive issue in the northern hemisphere than the issue of pro-life versus pro-choice. He went on to invite all of those in New America who did not accept this policy to emigrate. This pronouncement was welcomed by the Christian Right in the new nation and in the United States. Their joy was premature as they would soon learn.

His presentation was very deliberate, without any anger or indication of "toughness", in a very casual manner. He would maintain this same composure throughout his speech.

He proclaimed an immediate halt to all immigration into the nation. In recognition of the fact that there were many legal and illegal aliens within the borders of the new country, he also stated that they would not be eligible for citizenship and would, in due time, be deported. The President stated that his position on this subject was based on managing the manpower resources of the nation. All job preferences would be extended to native residents of the new nation. The penalties for businesses, farmers, and others who hired aliens would be severe. In addition to monetary penalties, the new nation would take control of the businesses that violated the law.

This policy was formulated for the President by a group of representatives from the radical far right. They never were enchanted with the immigration policies of the United States. In particular, they objected to the lax controls over the immigration into the United States of people from Central and South America, Africa, the Middle and Far East, Asia, and the South Pacific region. No doubt, they were very discriminating against people of color. It became even more evident when they did not raise the same objections to immigrants from central Europe and Scandinavia.

This policy would cause tremendous hardships on many aliens. These were people who migrated to North America with the objective of improving their lives and the lives of their families. Dreams would be shattered. No doubt the United States and even citizens of New America would protest this policy, but to no avail. The President had locked the policy in concrete. He was truly a pawn in the hands of the radical far right, including the militias. All of these followers in the United States who were listening to this announcement raised their glasses to toast the President. The Christian Right and many of the pro-life supporters, regardless of their political leanings or faith, were shocked at this announcement. It was contrary to their policies. This would have a dramatic impact on their followers and certainly on any attempts to convert the masses of people throughout the world. It seemed like a nightmare. Unfortunately, it was real.

The people in the United States and the world were shocked by this proclamation. Members of the United Nations protested the action to no avail. It was the only nation on earth that would institute such a policy. The foreign governments who provided financial support to the CCP began to have second thoughts about their actions. But, it was too late to change the course of events.

Even the leaders of the CCP and Republican Parties in the United States were shocked by the President's announcement. They too, began to wonder what evil they had helped to develop.

Their regrets would mount with the further pronouncements of the extreme policies of the President of New America.

The announcement that the new nation would not have any welfare programs was a shock to even the citizens of New America. This was a furtherance of the extreme right wing's philosophies. Their ideas on pro-life, immigration, and welfare were really well known for many years. But no one could imagine the application of policies such as these being proclaimed by the President. He continued to expound on the need for all individuals to accept responsibility for their livelihood. No one need turn to the State for welfare. The President projected the theme that the economy would provide work for every person in the nation. People who were handicapped would find employment within their capabilities. Companies would be encouraged to hire persons with disabilities. In turn, they would be eligible for certain tax benefits. But, every person would be given the opportunity to be self-sufficient.

This would be the only place on the globe that would have such stringent welfare policies. Many citizens of New America realized that things would never be the same in what was once the great State of Maine. Many began to wonder what other new policies were about to unfold. Many listeners became depressed. The night was still young. The President was only half finished with his pronouncements of policies applicable to the new nation.

The subject of gun controls was addressed briefly. There would be no gun controls. The gun lobby and militias had won.

The people of New America, as a group, enjoyed hunting, fishing, and other sports. They had no problem with this policy. To the contrary, they felt somewhat relieved at the announcement. This was the first good news that came out of the President's speech. The militias were especially happy. This would permit their members to arm themselves uncontrolled. Any type of weapons, i.e., automatic, semi-automatic, even mortars, could and would become part of their arsenals. They would in fact function as the military reserves for the new nation. This policy was in fact the payment for supporting the President.

The militias in the United States, who were organizationally connected to their counterparts in New America, were celebrating the developments.

The President was not finished with his radical announcements. There was still more to come.

The President addressed the subject of labor unions. He stated that he believed in labor unions. But, and with the same breath, he also stated that the nation had to be on guard against corruption in the labor movement. Accordingly, he stated that the policy of New America would be to control the organization and status of labor unions. Effective immediately, all existing labor organizations would be illegal. Only one labor union would be permitted to function in the Nation. A Government controlled labor union would be established. All labor related aspects would be controlled by the directors of the Government managed labor union. All negotiations between management and labor would be conducted by the Government. The controls would be total. This policy was formulated for the President by elements from the far right.

The announcement shocked all union leaders in the Nation and throughout the world. This was truly dictatorial. The listening audience was once again flabbergasted at this news. No one could imagine that the President would go this far in extending the policies that were associated with the extreme right wing elements. But, they were presented without the President even flinching. As they would soon learn, no amount of protests would change this policy. The lines were drawn by the President and his advisors. The latter came from the ranks of the far right including members of the militias. The CCP leadership had no input into these pronouncements. In fact, the CCP leadership was advised to cease and desist from attempting to influence the President. The tide had turned.

The shoe would fall with the final domestic pronouncement by the President. All previous pronouncements would pale in comparison. The citizens of the world would wonder if the times had returned to the Hitler era.

The President announced that all political parties in New America would be banned effective immediately. The only organization that would function as a "Political Party" would be the National Government Party (NGP). The head of this new Party would be the President of New America. All political office holders would automatically be members in the Party. The membership would extend to the appointed military chiefs of the new nation. NGP would control all political activities in the country. This control would extend over all decisions involving domestic policies. There was no doubt that this would extend to planning and controlling the education programs in the country. Obviously, this would mean that control would be exercised over schools of higher learning, such as colleges, and who would be able to attend these schools. Yes, it was reminiscent of the Hitler era. The pattern was similar. Hopefully, the results would not prove as disastrous to the new nation's citizens.

The leadership of the CCP knew that they had been betrayed. They realized that they were used by the extreme right wing of the United States. They could never realize the extent of the actions the President of New America would venture. It was a disaster. Unfortunately, it could not be undone. The CCP leadership realized that they had to acknowledge to the people of the United States their role in creating this monster. This was not an easy task. It was difficult to admit to the world that they had been duped. They were paying a terrible price for their acceptance of radical right wing elements in their struggles for pro-life. Their original cause, no matter how valid or righteous, became a shield for the radical right wing and other devious elements of society for accomplishing their own objectives.

World reaction was swift. The United Nations condemned the new nation. It called upon the United States to retake possession of the "Maine". However, the UN leadership was cognizant of the American President's role in the development of events. The President and members of Congress who associated with the Christian Right were shocked at the turn of events. They attempted to contact the President of New America to discuss softening his stance on the many areas of controversy. There was no response. It was a waiting game. The strategy had backfired on the members who originally supported the secession.

In the weeks following the President's declarations to the world of his domestic policies, he proceeded to publish additional decrees that applied to the new nation. The death penalty would be imposed for any capital crime, for example, murder, rape, armed robbery that resulted in the death of the victim, kidnapping, and crimes against the State. The last was purposely left nebulous. There were other announcements that related to taxes, voting rights, and similar domestic type issues. None were as earth shaking as those presented on September 1 to a world audience.

On October 1, the President addressed the world again. This time it was on the foreign policies of New America. Due to the radical domestic policies proclaimed on September 1, the world was tuned in to the President to determine the nature of his foreign policies. Everyone wondered if his foreign policies would equal or even come near to the shocking proclamations that he announced in relation to his domestic policies. They would be pleasantly surprised.

The President even changed the format of his foreign policy speech. He spoke in general terms and did not itemize.

The President's trade policies were extremely liberal to the foreign governments. He announced that there would be no trade tariffs. Foreign nations were encouraged to open trade offices in New America. The sole requirement placed on them was that they would hire local citizens in their offices. This would permit the continued high employment in the country. The President was especially solicitous of the reaction of the United States in respect to any trade embargo or sanctions that might be imposed on his nation. He realized that he needed to take every action to attract foreign money into the nation. This employment requirement, as minor as it might appear, would provide employment and foreign capital in the new nation. Every angle was going to be explored to encourage foreign investments in the nation's economy.

In addition to free trade, the President removed all air and sea port taxes of foreign ships, planes, and passengers entering New America. Every effort would be made to encourage foreign tourists into the country. The nation's forests and long sea coast made it ideal for outdoor sports. It was smart to capitalize on the natural resources of the country.

The President established a special office similar to the Commerce Department in the United States. It was addressed as simply the "Foreign Trade Office". The mission of this office was clearly defined in respect to foreign trade. It was to visit overseas areas and describe the products and services that could be purchased from New America.

The President identified the principal exports of New America in his speech, i.e., agricultural and dairy products. Both of these would attract foreign capital. The United States would be considered as a potential market. New America opened its fishing waters to foreign vessels in consideration of a small annual fee. Many nations, such as Japan, were more than willing to pay the fee in return for the fishing rights. From the Japanese point of view, it was a bargain.

The new nation would take advantage of its scenic coastline and vast forests to entice tourists from overseas and the United States. Its coastline of approximately 230 miles provided outstanding recreation activities. The Foreign Trade Office would institute an educational program for all of its citizens involving the manners and courtesies that should be exercised to its outside visitors. A movie film would be produced showing and narrating the nation's beautiful areas. The film would be taken to various nations for showing thereby introducing potential travellers to the advantages of visiting the new nation. The program would prove very rewarding.

The President ended his speech without the fanfare that accompanied his domestic policy speech. The world was now aware of the policies of New America. They were still in shock over the domestic policies. However, no one outside of the New America could be more taken back by the announcements than the CCP.

For all practical purposes, the new nation was capable of sustaining itself. With a population of roughly 1.2 million inhabitants, this effort was easily accomplished. The problem was the loss of freedom that the citizens would have as a result of the nation's policies.

The citizens of New America had difficulty in accepting the dictatorial actions of the Presidency. There was little that they could do. The members of the radical right wing and the militias were equivalent to the gestapo and SS of the Hitler era in Germany during the 20th century. Any gathering of citizens, such as farmers, store clerks, and others, would have members of the right wing or militia present. No discussion could take place involving protests of the Administration policies without the danger of the participants being reported to the police. There was no doubt that a police state existed in New America.

In the months to come, the citizens who disagreed with the policies of the nation began to emigrate. It was simple for them to cross the border into New Hampshire. There, they would seek asylum as political refugees. This was a dramatic action. The border police of New America did not stop any person wanting to leave the country. To the contrary, they encouraged all who did not agree with the President to emigrate. This same policy was applied to any resident who was not Caucasian. There was no doubt that the nation exercised a policy of racism. It did not end with racism. Persons of other religious beliefs were encouraged by more subtle means to leave the country. Many did so. However, others would stay and try to live with the conditions. If there was any good aspect of these actions, it was the fact that the nation did not resort to violence against those who had conflicts with the President and the policies of New America.

The foreign governments did do business with New America. They were very skeptical. Based on the domestic policies of the new nation, they were aware of the hypocrisy of the President and the government. Neither could be trusted.

Some foreign governments were overjoyed with the developments in the new country. The entire episode was viewed as a blow against the United States. The foreign governments were initially baffled by the lack of action on the part of the United States to undo what had occurred. They fully anticipated that the United States would not allow any of its States to secede from the Union. The fact that they did allow this to happen was certainly seen as a weakness in the democratic system. They were more shocked that the United States did nothing even after the President of New America announced his domestic policies.

Some of the foreign governments channeled secret funds into the treasury of the new nation. It was their way of encouraging the split between New America and the United States.

The American government would, through its own secret channels, learn of these developments in time. In the interim the monies would flow freely from overseas into the new nation.

The President of New America accepted the foreign money without any reservations. The country needed external financial assistance if it was to survive. Operating the government would by itself require great sums of money. In addition, the new nation would need financial resources for maintenance of highways, public buildings, and for operating the schools. Income taxes alone could not support the new nation.

The citizens of New America lived day by day. They were thankful that they were employed and did not have to go hungry. Their stomachs were full. The same could not be said for their spirits. The controls were stifling. Many did accept the policies of their President. There were those who were against immigration, integration, and unions. A large number of citizens were pro-life and strong anti pro-choice. And yet many others were against welfare. However, these same individuals felt caged. Being against something, but having the freedom to do so, they discovered was totally different from being forbidden by law. It was certainly a contradiction at the highest level. It boggled the mind and caused much mental stress. The weak nervous systems reacted quickly.

There were those who were in favor of some of the President's policies but who took exception to others. They too had a dilemma. What to do? If they were pro-life but favored free labor unions and nondiscriminatory policies, their consciences were troubled. Many, without being cognizant, were in fact reliving the experiences of the Christian Coalition Party in the United States. The CCP closed their eyes to the radical right wing and militias. Could the citizens of New America do the same? Each individual would be required to address the issue.

Many knew the outcome of the CCP closing its eyes to the problem.

The citizens of New America were bombarded with propaganda from the government relative to the many advantages they, as a new nation, would realize from the nation's domestic and foreign policies. The television and radio stations, controlled by the government, saturated the air waves daily with tales of the good life in the country. What they did not reveal were the number of its citizens who emigrated, had nervous break-downs, and who committed suicide out of frustration and the inability to cope with the pressures of the system.

The President of the United States and key members of Congress, all members of the Christian Right, met to review the developments in New America. Being aware of how they were manipulated by the radical right wing and militias, they tried to ascertain if there was any way that they could undo the developments. The consensus was that unless they wanted to have civil disobedience and even the possibility of a civil war, there was little if anything that they could do at this time. They were totally aware that the President and his staff of New America had strong and influential followers in the United States. The numerous State militias, who were heavily armed, were a real source of potential troubles. The fanatic supporters of anti-gun control, anti-welfare, anti-unions, anti-immigration, and, yes, anti-abortion were strong in the United States. Any one of these groups could overreact to any military action that the United States would take against New America. They decided that military action was not an option. They had helped create this monster, now they had to try to do something to stop it in its tracks.

After long deliberations, they decided that their best strategy would be to use peaceful means to solve the problem. The domestic radical policies of the new nation were the problem. It was decided that the President would appoint a committee comprised of CCP members to visit Augusta and the President of New America with the mission of having the radical domestic issues softened. Yes, keep the ideals in force. But, remove the threat of criminal actions and remove the laws that prohibit labor unions, immigration, integration, and other political parties. Also, reinstitute welfare as deemed appropriate. The announced policy on abortions could remain in place. After all, this was the key element in the CCP charter for years. It was believed that these were all worthy objectives of the committee. More important they were practical and would probably undo the public relations disaster that was incurred on September 1.

It was decided that the committee would move quickly to make arrangements to meet with the President of New America.

A meeting was scheduled on this action in Augusta for November 1. The committee, comprised of CCP officials, felt very confident in accomplishing their mission.

The President of New America met with his principal advisors on the eve of November 1. They had been informed of the mission of the committee from Washington. Their contacts in the White House and in Congress, including the CCP, provided details on the visiting committee's objectives. There was no secret to the mission from Washington. Preparations were made to listen to the presenters. The reclama would be made immediately thereafter. No potential problems were foreseen.

The committee from Washington received a very cordial welcome. They were treated and dined like foreign dignitaries. After all, they had many things in common. They all shared some common interests, particularly on the abortion issue. The meeting progressed rapidly. The presentation of the D.C. group took a few hours. The advantages were cited for the administration of New America in accepting the recommended domestic policy changes. No changes were submitted relating to the foreign policy of New America. The meeting was interrupted for lunch.

At lunch, the President of New America and his staff were very gracious. There was no indication of their feelings on the morning's discussions. The group from Washington could not read anything in the action or lack of action of the President or any of his staff.

The President opened the afternoon session by extending his appreciation for the committee's visit, their recommendations and their concerns with the policies of the new nation. He did

102

expound on the similarities of issues that concerned both New America and the United States.

He did remind the visitors, albeit so gently, that New America was a sovereign nation. As such, it reserved the right to establish such domestic and foreign policies that were consistent with the wishes of its people. Accordingly, even though he and his staff appreciated their concerns and recommendations, New America would not change its announced policies. And with that, he wished them well. He extended his greetings to his many friends in Washington, including the President of the United States. As an afterthought, he indicated that he hoped both countries would continue to work in harmony and left the room.

The committee returned to Washington to report to the President of the United States and the principal members of the CCP.

CHAPTER 8

THE IMPACT ON THE AMERICAN CONTINENT

The world accepted the new nation of New America, The impact of the action would haunt the American Continent. Every nation from Canada to the tip of South America would in some form feel the effects of the action. The entire continent could only sit back and observe the further unfolding of this drama. The governments and people were amazed that this could happen in the United States.

No doubt the United States was facing the greatest challenge to its survival as a world power, both economically and militarily. The President of the United States and his principal staff were acutely aware of the impact of the secession of the State of Maine. They were active parties in developing the strategies that would eventually result in embarrassing the nation on a grandiose scale. If this were the only impact of their mistake, they could be excused. But, the eventual developments that followed were unpardonable. The radical right wing of the Republican Party in concert with the many militant militias scattered throughout the country made fools of the CCP leadership and many of their followers from all walks of life. The devious act and betrayal of the extremists took advantage of the Christian Right and its pro-life issue. The CCP knew it made a mistake in trusting the many diverse participants to its cause. It was too late to undo the act.

The CCP would lose considerable power and leverage as a result of the developments. Prior to the secession, the CCP dominated the American political scene. In coordination with the Republican Party, they literally controlled the destiny of the United States. As time progressed following the secession, both the CCP and the Republican Party lost influence with the American voters.

The Democratic Party gained power at the expense of the CCP. Together with the Freedom and Social Scientist Parties, the Democrats formed a coalition that would compete with the CCP and Republican Parties in local, state, and national elections. The political scene in the United States changed overnight. No one wanted a repeat of what happened with the former State of Maine. The rallying cry of the Democrats in all elections was, "Remember Maine". This was a historical phrase that was reintroduced with a slight twist. It worked wonders on the voters.

Canada had a dilemma. On one hand, it had its own "Quebec" incident that occurred late in the 20th century. Some French speaking citizens, backed by France, wanted to have the Province separated from Canada. Independence was the goal. Fortunately, common sense prevailed and nothing happened. Canada remained united but the threat of Quebec seceding from the nation never disappeared entirely. The problem lingered through the years.

This experience by the Canadians provided them with first hand knowledge of the real and potential problems that a nation faces when confronted with secession by one of its numbers. The close relationship between the Canadian Government and the American Government, including the personal contacts between the Canadian Prime Minister and the President of the United States, presented the Canadians with a very unusual set of circumstances. On one hand, the citizens of Quebec were very sympathetic with the plight of New America. They were cognizant of the need of the new nation for all sorts of outside support. However, they were also aware of the problems Washington faced in dealing with the secession. What to do? Who to support? These were only a few of the myriad of questions facing not only the Canadian Government but also its citizens. Time might provide some answers. However, the problem was not going go away.

Officially the Canadian Government took the position after discussions with the Americans that they would establish relations with the new nation of New America in the same manner as if it were a nation on another continent. This policy seemed to have favor with the people of Canada.

Certainly the President of New America welcomed the relationship. The situation was better than he could have imagined.

The feelings and attitudes of the Mexican Government toward the new developments on the continent were diametrically different from Canada. There was no doubt that this could be traced to the domestic policies announced by the President of the new nation. This plus the subsequent deportation of Mexican nationals who had immigrated to Maine years ago and were waiting for their citizenship papers to be processed caused the Mexican Government to withhold recognition of the new nation. The Mexican Government was aware of the racist attitudes of some Americans. It also realized that the President of New America was anti-immigration and, in earlier years while still in the United States, openly announced his anti-Mexican feelings. Discriminating against Mexicans was traced back to his statements and policies that suggested Washington should close the borders with Mexico to stem the tide of immigrants.

Under the circumstances, there could not be a friendly relationship between the two nations. The majority of Mexicans agreed entirely with their Government's action. They would endorse the statements of the President of Mexico.

A movement took place, although of no significance, to block any imports from the new nation. For all practical purposes this was a meaningless gesture. But, it served its political purpose in Mexico. The people were placated. Mexico would never recognize the new nation.

Other countries in Central America, for example, Panama and Costa Rica, were not impacted directly by the developments in North America. However, the secession of Maine from the United States was significant from a status point of view. The prestige of the American continent was adversely impacted. Prior to the secession of Maine from the United States, the American continent was considered special. A continent that thrived by any measurement. The United States, in particular, led the world in every measurable facet.

Led by the United States, the entire continent thrived economically. The military strength of the American continent, led by the United States, was unequaled on earth.

The freedoms enjoyed by all the citizens of the continent were the envy of the world. The United States, in particular, had gained the reputation of the "great melting pot" of various racial, ethnic, and religious groups. Even so, many people wondered if the Americans enjoyed too much freedom. There were the issues of gun control, constant arguments on immigration and, of course, the pro-life versus the pro-choice controversy that caused turmoil.

With all factors considered, the governments and people of Central America believed that they too were losers in the happenings in the United States. They considered themselves a partner of the United States. Anything that happened on the continent, especially in the United States, had an impact on their lives. They were correct in this assessment.

There was no doubt that countries like Mexico, Panama, and Costa Rica would feel the effects of the action that took place in the north. First and foremost, the tourism business would decrease. The Central Americans would be reluctant to visit the United States. The relationship of the Christian Right Party with New America was well known. The policies enunciated by the President of New America involving immigration were considered discriminatory to put it mildly. The existence of armed militias and their known stance against people of different races was not overlooked. It was not too difficult to recognize why the people were reluctant to visit the northern hemisphere.

The Americans were leery to tour Central America. They were alarmed to read that a few tourists who visited Mexico and Panama were threatened with bodily harm. Certainly they were discouraged from remaining in the area.

The export and import trade also suffered. Next to tourism, foreign trade between the United States and Central America was the second largest business activity. The people refused to purchase items from New America. Conversely, many businesses did not want to do business with the Americans. This was true even though high prices were offered, particularly for agricultural products in the winter months.

No nation in Central America would recognize the new nation.

The countries of South America had reactions similar to Central America. They could not understand how the United States could have permitted the secession to take place. They were very familiar with the historical turmoil that occurred in Central and South America. The many revolutions, civil wars, and dictatorships that the countries of these regions endured were well documented. The drug cartels that operated openly for decades were a thorn in the side of most of the nations in Central and South America. Most, if not all, of these problems were directly and indirectly associated with poverty amongst the citizens. This was somewhat understandable. In addition, the nations of the area were controlled by a minority of the population. Graft and corruption prevailed in almost every nation of the region. However, in recent years, tremendous gains had been made in establishing honest governments and democracies. The drug cartels were removed. Graft and corruption, although not totally done away with, were controlled.

Many of the problems in earlier years, especially drugs, were the direct result of the American markets. The demand for drugs in the United States in the late 20th century and early part of the 21st century was the driving force behind the drug trade. However, this activity was also responsible for much of the turmoil in those countries including the political graft and corruption. Fortunately, this illicit drug business ended and with it many of the other problems.

Subsequently, the nations of South America joined the United States and the rest of the world in enjoying the fruits of the global market. The times were never better for the citizens of the area.

The impact of the action that took place in the United States would do nothing to enhance the quality of life of the people of South America. Much of their lives were directly entangled with the activities of the Americans. Their economies were, for the most part, dependent on the Americans. Similar to the economy

109

of Central America, the countries of South America depended on tourism and the export/import business involving the Americans. This represented over 80 per cent of their gross national product. Any reduction in business with the United States would directly impact the economies of South America. It was no wonder that they were concerned with the actions in the United States.

Again like the people of Central America, the South Americans recognized the nature of the beast in control of New America. The policies of the new nation were abundantly clear. There was no doubt that the new nation had discriminatory policies that impacted the South Americans. The people of the region presented a solid front opposing any relations with the new nation. In fact, they also questioned the sincerity of the government of the United States.

South America decided that no matter what the cost to their economy, they would not recognize New America. They would not engage in any foreign trade with the nation. In fact, they would question their relationship with the United States.

The developments in the United States, in particular the secession of Maine, would cause turmoil throughout the Americas.

The President of the United States soon learned of the reactions of the governments from Canada, Central and South America. He realized in all of the planning, no one from Group X or the subsequent committee established to develop the strategy and time-table for the secession had considered the impact of the action on the nations in their own backyard. It was a revelation. Needless to say, the entire American Congress was in turmoil. The CCP leaders were shocked.

Many of the Congressional leaders were dependent on campaign support, including funds, from various ethnic and racial groups. Many of whom had Central and South American heritage. They were shocked at the quick and radical reactions of many of their constituents. Coping with a potential political disaster would not be an easy task. It would require all of the political savvy they possessed to deal with the problem. It was a race against time. Many of those contacting Washington had already indicated that they were dropping their support of the

President and changing Party affiliations. The Congressmen recognized the severity of the problem.

The Congressional leaders from the CCP and Republican Party contacted the White House, attempting to arrange a meeting to discuss the crisis. The President's aides were quick to respond. A special meeting was scheduled with the leaders of both political Parties to discuss the problems caused by the secession of Maine and the declaration of the domestic policies by the President. of New America. It would be a chaotic meeting. The Congressmen were in a demanding mood. They knew that something had to be done to settle the situation, but they themselves had no solution. They looked to the President of the United States for a solution to their dilemma.

The President had a difficult time attempting to still the outbursts from the Congressmen. Everyone was talking at the same time. The President was shocked. Not at the chaos but rather at the lack of courtesy to the President. They spared no words in blaming him for their problems. He did, however, realize that the situation was serious. When the Party was losing supporters, especially financial supporters, it was not a trivial matter. The meeting lasted for six hours. It was scheduled for thirty minutes.

After all the shouting and name calling was over, the President attempted to pacify the Congressional members by suggesting that he could invite the President of New America to Washington to meet with them and himself to discuss the problems that emanated from his domestic policies. This seemed to settle the group. However, some pointed out that the meeting was urgent in view of current events. The tide of dissentions increased daily. It was not a meeting that could be put off for weeks.

The President and the members of Congress were unanimous in believing that events could not be undone. They recognized that the problem associated with New America was self inflicted. The fact that the President of New America, even though hand picked by the CCP leadership, had his own agenda once the new nation was established was a moot point at this time. Accordingly, the meeting adjourned with no real solutions to the problem other than the scheduled action to invite the President of New America to Washington.

The President of New America was accompanied by a select few from his staff on his visit to Washington. The meeting between he, the President of the United States, and the CCP leadership was conducted in the White House. The President of New America would not change his position on any established policies. The meeting adjourned within one hour of starting, The President of New America and his staff returned to Augusta the same day.

The secession of Maine from the United States and the subsequent declaration of domestic and foreign policies by the President of the new nation would alter the political and business relationships between all of the nations on the continent and the United States and its new neighbor, New America.

CHAPTER 9

NEW AMERICA'S PROBLEMS

New America's problems began the day it was born. Perhaps the President, the leaders of the new nation, and its citizens were too involved in celebrating its independence to recognize the troubles that come with independence.

The citizens of New America had mixed reactions to their new status. The fact that the CCP and Republican Party had encouraged many of their members to relocate to the State of Maine in earlier years in preparation for the secession from the United States provided a nucleus of support within the state. Many of its citizens were prepared for the action. However, there were many native citizens who traced their history in the State several generations and who were totally surprised by the development of events. All of the people of the new nation wondered how their lives would be impacted by their new status. The answers would come soon enough.

The domestic policies of the new nation were welcomed by some of the citizens. The majority of the people disagreed with the radical policies involving immigration, labor unions, and the severity of the rules governing the welfare programs. The strong position taken on the abortion issue was surprising. Also, the penalties involving some of the capital crimes were believed by many to be too severe. Overall, however, the people were not overly concerned with the developments. There were some worse things to appear in time.

Initially the people had no problem existing. Jobs and food were plentiful. No one was without work or food. Most goods and supplies that the people required to sustain themselves were available. Shortages of some items began to appear after about six months. At the beginning, this was not considered a serious matter. Most everyone believed that it was a temporary situation.

Prior to the secession, the State of Maine depended on many items from other parts of the United States and foreign nations. New America would require the same capability. There were no heavy industries located in the new nation. The country would continue to be totally dependent on outside sources for appliances, automobiles, some data processing hardware and software, farm equipment, and similar goods. Prior to the secession, all such items that were shipped into the State of Maine were taken for granted. This was no longer the case. The new nation would be totally dependent on imports for items not produced in New America. The process would take its toll. The nation did not have the means, financial or otherwise, to develop its own capabilities, that is, to become self sufficient in satisfying the needs of its citizens.

Soon, too soon, shortages developed in spare parts for appliances, automobiles, farm equipment, and other similar products. It was reminiscent of the shortages that occurred in Cuba in the late 20th century after the United States imposed a blockade in connection with the Cuban missile crisis. A black market developed overnight in spare parts. It was a throw back to "Indian trading". People would barter with different items for something they needed. Some would trade clothing for tools. Others would exchange furniture for automobile parts. A barter system developed in the new nation. The population was becoming irritable. This was only the beginning of the numerous problems that would face the people of New America.

The time approached when the spare parts would not satisfy the needs. New equipment, appliances, cars, and various tools were in short supply and desperately needed to sustain the economy. All of these hard goods needed to be imported. The costs would increase accordingly. The consumers were becoming restless. They began to complain, but to no avail. There was no one to take complaints. Criticizing the State in public could be dangerous. No one knew who to trust. Neighbors became suspicious of each other. Life was becoming a challenge.

The citizens of New America longed for the good old days. A time when they were able to satisfy all of their needs. If the goods were not available locally, they could drive into New Hampshire or other nearby States and make their purchases. They could also drive to Canada to buy and satisfy their needs. Prices were reasonable at that time. Life was comfortable. This was no longer the case. The quality of life began to deteriorate rapidly.

Many citizens had friends and relatives in the United States. As embarrassing as it was, they had no choice but to ask for help from the outside. It became a ridiculous situation. It was like asking for foreign assistance. To those who had no other choice but to request help from friends and relatives in the United States, it was no laughing matter. In all instances, it was a case of survival. Without this assistance, even financial help, some families would be destitute. They were on a downward spiral. The population became disenchanted with the developments.

The export/import business did not blossom as anticipated by the President of the new nation. Many potential foreign suppliers were skeptical of the ability of New America to pay for its imports. On the other hand, the nation's exports were extremely limited.

The lack of imports posed a major problem to the new nation. The survival of the new country would depend on its ability to import the necessary supplies and equipment to maintain a healthy economy. The fact that the nation could not sustain itself on its domestic products alone was troubling. The currency problem was real. The President decided at the outset that the nation's monetary system would be the American dollar. He had no choice. The lack of a sound economy did not help the situation. As time progressed, the problem compounded. More nations refused to extend credit to the new nation.

The lack of exports had an effect on every aspect of the new nation. It could not balance its costs of imports. The exports did not generate the income expected. Agricultural products, timber, and tourism were not that great. The revenues were inadequate in order to balance the foreign trade. It did help the economy but ever so lightly. There were no big ticket items or products that could generate a greater inflow of funds into the nation.

The domestic policies announced by the President contributed immeasurably to the nation's economic problems. Few nations were anxious to do business with the country. Some nations, those who gained from the downfall of the United States (at least in reputation) made significant loans to the new nation.

The loans were to be repaid with goods and services provided by New America. This was a very acceptable arrangement. A few nations who wanted total secrecy provided financial grants to the new nation. These were nations who enjoyed seeing the United States squander their world status. They were also the same nations who waited for an opportunity to start aggressive actions against their neighbors. The danger lurked in Africa and the Middle East. New America not only had its immediate internal problems but was also contributing to the future instability of the world. It seemed there was no end in sight to the problems of New America.

The problems that New America had with the rest of the world paled in comparison to its problems with the United States. The President of the United States, the American Congress, and the American people all were against providing any assistance to the new nation. The President was forced to take many actions against the new neighbor. Violence was not part of the solution. The same tactics that might be used against a foreign power would be employed against New America.

One of the first actions was to establish strong border guards on all roads leading into and out of the new nation. It was a mini-blockade. The move was more harassing than anything else. It was to show the attitude of the President of the United States toward the new nation's leadership. It worked wonders. If nothing else, the move was heralded by members of Congress and the American people. The President had no choice but to take actions, even though they were not considered drastic, against New America. The United States was losing prestige around the globe. The American people demanded some action against what they considered to be an illegitimate secession. The President was facing political turmoil.

The plight of the citizens of New America, including their shortages and hardships, was continuously exploited by the White House. The press conferences of the President of the United States were scheduled more frequently than normal. He would always make it point to expound on the trials and tribulations of the citizens of the new nation. The citizens of

New America were listening to these broadcasts. The news was not falling on deaf ears.

The President of New America knew what was happening. It was beyond his control to stop. He turned loose the tigers when he turned his back on the American President and Congress in their meeting in Washington, D.C. It was payback time. The problems of New America were just beginning.

The President of New America called a meeting of his staff to review the condition of the country. He wanted a total analysis of the events that occurred since the day of independence of their nation. He called for honest and blunt comments. The responses were shocking.

Each of his appointed staff criticized the direct approach the nation had taken in announcing their domestic and foreign policies. There was no doubt in the minds of every person attending the meeting that it was a blunder that would prove costly to the nation. The emphasis of the criticism was on the extreme right wing pronouncements involving the issues of immigration, welfare, gun controls, labor unions, and the right to life. Even though these positions were valid in so far as the nation's leadership was concerned, the entire staff agreed that it was a mistake to publicly state the President's policies on these issues.

All present at the meeting also agreed that the nation was headed for economic collapse unless something drastic happened to change the tide. But no one presented a solution to the problem. How to change the course of events remained an open question. The President of New America had no solutions to the problems that he had and his fellow extremists created since the secession.

The President requested the staff to return to their offices and to give priority consideration to developing ideas that the country could use in reversing its course. With this, the President dismissed the staff and returned to his office to contemplate his predicament.

The problems encountered by the citizens of New America began to take their toll. A population of approximately 1.3 million citizens began to drop in numbers. The President's encouragement of legal and illegal immigrants to leave the country was taken to heart by thousands. In addition, citizens of various racial backgrounds began to leave the nation due to its open discriminatory policies. This resulted in thousands of people of color leaving the country, Many departed for Canada, Still others crossed the border into Vermont. From there, they relocated to various parts of the United States.

Many of the people who emigrated were professionals. Doctors, lawyers, engineers, and academicians were among those leaving New America. They realized that the future of the nation was bleak.

The general population was becoming nervous. The failing economy, hardships that were becoming more visible, and the exodus of professionals from the work force were duly noted. This caused many native inhabitants to leave the country. They too crossed the borders into Canada and the United States. The trickle began to turn into a deluge of citizens moving out of the new nation. Shortly, the population of New America fell below 900,000. There was chaos in Augusta.

Some of the President's advisors could only see something good from the emigration. They were short sighted. They did not take cognizance of the fact that the majority of the people leaving the country were the elite. Again, this was reminiscent of the Hitler era in Germany when that nation discarded many of its professional citizens, many of whom migrated to the United States and assisted immeasurably in helping to defeat the axis powers. History was repeating itself. New America was moving deeper into troubled waters.

CHAPTER 10

THE NEW UNITED STATES

A new era was beginning in the United States. The citizens of the country knew what had happened. The entire story of the President's role, the CCP, and the extreme right wing in the scheming that was involved in the secession of Maine from the United States was published and made know by the news media. The power of both the CCP and the Republican Party diminished overnight. The Democratic Party was joined by the Freedom and Social Scientist Parties to form a solid coalition against the CCP and Republican Party. To add insult to injury to the President and the leaders of the CCP and Republican Party, many of their members switched their allegiance to the Democratic Party. Many were shocked when the details became known of the CCP and Republican Party participation in the secession of Maine. The news could not be restrained. The only elements that remained totally dedicated to the Republican and CCP cause were the state militias. They were the hard core of the far right.

Impeachment proceedings against the President were initiated but were never culminated. The leaders of the Democratic, Freedom, and Social Scientist Parties recognized the turmoil caused by the secession throughout the nation. They agreed that pursuing the impeachment action would no doubt be successful. However, they also agreed that the procedures and time involved would extract too heavy a price on the citizens of the country. Such an action could only add to the grief and frustrations already existing in the public arena.

The Democrats, together with their allies prepared for the next state and national elections. There was much work to be done. The elections in 2032 would be historic. Every state in the country would register record numbers of voters. Subsequently, voters would turn out in record numbers. Voter apathy was a thing of the past. The Americans had learned a lesson the hard way. Voter apathy had cost them a State.

The people of the United States, at least for the immediate future, accepted the secession of Maine and the establishment of the new nation. The action had no significant impact on the nation's economy. The employment picture continued to be excellent. National unemployment was less than 6 per cent. This was close to the preceding years. Inflation was less than 4 per cent annually. The people of the United States were having a good life. As always, the American people paid little, if any, attention to what the foreign nations thought about the United States. It would take time before they would realize the entire world was always watching what occurred in the United States. After all, the nation was the world's leading economic and military power even with all of its internal problems. Everything that happened in the United States made international news. The secession of Maine was certainly in the category of a major development and would make the news headlines in every nation on earth. Most foreigners could not believe that the American people took the secession so calmly and without major protests. In many other countries, the action would lead to civil war.

The nation's economy continued to grow. Fortunately, the President of the United States did maintain a strong Department of Defense. Nothing would change in this respect.

The global markets and free trade policies facilitated the nation to take full advantage of its research and development to maintain its lead in high technology, medical, manufacturing, and other fields. Of particular benefit was the nation's ability to produce agricultural products in record abundance to satisfy the demands of the world. The United States was fortunate to have a climate that permitted the farmers to grow crops almost year round. This coupled with the development of new and hybrid seeds permitted farmers to grow record crops. Universities and corporate farms took the lead in research and development to produce new crops and seeds that were resistant to disease, pests, and weather. The nation's food basket was bursting. This resulted in record breaking exports of agricultural products. Fortunately, this provided the necessary food to sustain a large portion of the world's population.

The annual income of the American factory worker was in the vicinity of $75,000 annually. This far exceeded the income of much of the world's labor force. This permitted the American worker to live very comfortably. Providing for the education of their children was no problem. The families enjoyed extensive vacations. It was not unusual for a working family to take two vacations a year, one in summer and one in the winter. Vacations to overseas destinations were normal. The American worker continued to be envied throughout the world. In this respect, the secession of Maine had no adverse impact.

The American workers had few if any problems with job security. They had no problem with the immigration of foreign labor into the country. The immigrants were eager to work. Just as important to the American economy, they contributed directly to the nation's ability to maintain a record low inflation.

The labor unions had no restrictions on organizing. They did, however, have difficulty in attracting new members. Employers were forced to provide fair wages and good benefits due to the competition for labor. Most unions had to be satisfied to retain the members that were on their rolls.

Companies in the United States advertised their acceptance of labor unions in New America. They used every available news media to do so with the objective of reaching many of the remaining skilled labor in the new nation. They were hoping that this would attract many to emigrate to the United States to help satisfy that nation's demand for their skills. This proved to be very successful. Unfortunately for New America, this action contributed significantly to the drain of its labor supply. Even many of the supposedly loyal supporters of the CCP emigrated to the United States. This loss of skilled labor caused a further erosion of the quality of life in New America. The problems of the new nation continued to mount.

In 2031, the political parties in the United States began to prepare for the 2032 state and national elections. It would be the most expensive political campaign in the history of the United States. Because none of the political parties took action to preclude the flow of foreign money into the United States arena, the 2032 elections would break all records of foreign money coming into the country. It seemed that every nation on earth had a valid reason for investing in the American elections.

The CCP and Republican Parties were way behind in the public polls. Based on every nonpartisan poll taken in 2031, the general public favored the Democrats by 55 percent, the Freedom Party by 15 per cent, and the Social Scientist Party by 10 percent. This coalition totaled 80 percent. Conversely, the CCP and Republican Parties combined were favored by 20 percent of the voters. This was dramatically different from the 2028 elections. The public polls made a full circle.

There was no question that the fiasco engineered by the CCP in coordination with the Republican Party that resulted in the secession of Maine was totally responsible for the turnaround of the voters. The leaders of the CCP and the Republican Party knew that they had a real struggle on their hands with the forthcoming election. The radical right wing of both parties made significant financial contributions to the campaign. There was no doubt in the minds of both political party leaders that much more money would be needed if they were to retain their state and national offices. This meant that foreign money, in great amounts, would need to be raised, and quickly. In order to meet this need, the President of the New America would visit overseas capitals to raise funds. All of this would be done under the pretense of State visits. He was so far in trouble at this stage, that this additional action could not make his position any worse.

The leader of the CCP also took it upon himself to solicit funds openly in his radio and television shows. These were supposedly religious programs. They dropped all pretense and concentrated on requesting listeners to send in campaign contributions for the forthcoming elections. The Chairman of the Republican Party travelled throughout the nation, attending political rallies, in an effort to raise campaign contributions.

None of these efforts were able to generate enough funds to change the polls. To the contrary, the two political parties lost ground. No amount of spending by the CCP and Republican Party could offset the adverse publicity that resulted from the secession of Maine from the United States. The people of the country were inundated with the details of the corruption that took place. There were many Americans who would probably not have objected as strenuously if the secession had taken place without the conniving of the CCP and Republican Party. The route that the action had taken was the cause of much bitterness. Many believed that leaders of the CCP and Republican Party, particularly the former, committed a grievous fraud against the American people. The secret meetings and agendas were unpardonable in the eyes of the voters. It appeared that no matter how much money was spent by the CCP and Republican Party, they would not be able to recapture the American voter's confidence of the year 2028.

The Democratic Party had no difficulty in raising campaign funds for the year 2032. To the contrary, the American public made record contributions to their cause. Something very unusual occurred during the year 2031. Unsolicited contributions were received in record breaking numbers and amounts. This was attributed to the rejections of the CCP and Republican Party, There was no doubt that the 2032 elections would belong to the Democrats and their FP and SSP supporters.

The problem that the Democrats had was working closely with the Freedom and Social Scientist Parties to assure that the best qualified candidates would be selected to run for the state and national offices. They all knew that the elections would be successful for their parties unless they did something very stupid. They certainly did not want to conduct any secret meetings or have any secret agendas. They went to extremes in inviting news media to their meetings and also invited the general public.

Every state in the country had candidates representing the Democrat's coalition. The campaigns were started in the fall of 2031.

By the spring of 2032, there was no question that the United States would be governed by a new regime. The Democrats would not only win the Presidency but also control both houses of Congress. Every state in the union would elect a governor from the Democratic, Freedom, or Social Scientist Party. This control also applied to the state houses. The days of the CCP and Republican Party came to an abrupt halt.

It appeared that the clock was moved back thirty years.

Everything in the United States seemed as though nothing had changed since the year 2000. The country was stable, the economy flourished, the balance of trade was favorable, and the employment factor was very acceptable.

The people of the nation had faith in their government. Most if not all voters realized that they had a major stake in all elections. Voter apathy would not be as widespread as in previous years. The people of the United States finally, at least for the time being, realized the costs to the nation when they neglect to vote.

The new leaders of the country made every attempt to retain the same freedoms that existed prior to the 2028 elections. They went out of their way to review and discuss openly the major differences of attitudes, opinions, and beliefs in the country.

The policies on immigration would remain unchanged. The nation as a whole, believed that its success was attributed to the influx of diverse people from all corners of the globe.

There was little question that it was this diversity that enabled the United States to exert tremendous influence on other nations having citizens of different racial, religious, and ethnic backgrounds. The country was living proof that such nations could live in peace,

The welfare system was managed with improved professional assistance. The system would provide a safety net for families having problems. Yes, this was extended to towns and cities that suffered from severe weather, such as tornadoes, hurricanes, and floods. This type of assistance was really associated with relief from the Federal Government. It was no different from the help to individuals or families in time of need.

The very complex and divisive issue of pro-life versus pro-choice was addressed. Emphasis was placed on individual rights. There were provisions for the pro-life advocates to publicize their goals and objections to the pro-choice group. Conversely, the pro-choice leaders were provided the same opportunities to voice their goals and position on the topic.

Basically, the beliefs of both sides were honored. The responsibility for one or the other view would depend on each side and its education program. It was believed that education on the subject was the best way to entice people to join one side or the other. What everyone hoped for, regardless of which side of the issue the people took, was that all violence would cease. This was preached to all citizens.

A major issue that remained to be solved in the United States was the question of militias. The leaders of the country, as well as the general population, did not object to the militias as long as their loyalty was to the United States. The American public did not want the militias to pose a threat to the nation's security. To assure that the militias would abide by these guide lines, Congress passed a law requiring that all militias register within the State in which they were located. The name of the militia, the number of members, and the list of its officers would suffice. Failure to register would be considered a felony. Further, failure to register would be construed as evidence that the militia was advocating the overthrow of the Government of the United States. This law was passed by Congress and signed by the President of the United States. The law was challenged by elements of the far right and the militias. The case was finally settled by the Supreme Court of the United States. The law was upheld, The Supreme Court held that the year 2033 was different from the periods of the 18th, 19th, and even part of the 20th centuries. Circumstances in the nation were totally different. The nation was living in a new era.

The new and rejuvenated United States was experiencing a revival that would continue for the foreseeable future. The international prestige that the nation enjoyed prior to the year 2028 began to return. Many foreign nations made direct contact with the White House to express their joy at the turn of events. Congratulations flooded the White House.

The people of the new United States had demonstrated to the world once again that they were intelligent voters. They could take credit for recognizing their previous shortfalls and have the courage and commitments to take corrective actions. The Americans were once again envied by the world.

CHAPTER 11

COEXISTENCE

The United States continued to enjoy prosperity. The free trade policies and global markets created a world-wide demand for American products. The American life style was very visible to the citizens of every nation on earth. The Americans were the envy of many nations.

Actions were taken by the United States Government in conjunction with private industry to create new industries and employment opportunities on other continents and particularly in undeveloped nations. The objective was to assist those nations to improve their economies and, in time, to provide new markets for American exports. This would also encourage the citizens of these nations to remain home and not migrate to other countries. The efforts of the Federal Government and private industry proved successful.

Close to home, the status of New America was reviewed by the leaders of the Democratic, Freedom, and Social Scientist Parties. It was decided to establish a joint working committee to evaluate what should be done with its neighbor, New America. The committee consisted of two representatives from each of the political parties. They were to study the situation and submit a report to the President of the United States in three months. Their charter provided for them to visit New America and establish talks with the President of New America and the leaders of the CCP and Republican Parties in the United States. The committee was provided office space at Ft. McNair, in Washington, D.C.

The committee had no problems arranging for meetings with the head of the CCP and Chairman of the Republican Party in the United States. Both were very eager to discuss the issue. Of main concern to the head of the CCP and the Chairman was the question of the nation's relationship with New America. Perhaps due to their own secret planning in bringing about the secession of Maine from the United States, they wondered what the plans were of the President of the United States and the leaders of the three political parties now in control of the destiny of both countries, the United States and New America.

The main question studied was what, if anything, should be done with New America? Should the United States Government reverse the decision of the former President and Congress that permitted the secession to take place? Would military force be used to undo the action? What penalties would the leaders of the action face? Would the law be extended to the CCP and Republican leaders who were responsible for the act?

If the secession would be permitted to continue without any action by the United States to rescind the separation, how should the United States treat the new nation? Should the United States institute a trade embargo? Should a blockade be placed on land and sea to force the leaders in New America to return to the United States?

These were serious questions that needed to be addressed by the committee. The committee's evaluations and recommendations would be critical.

The first meetings that took place between the committee and the leaders of the CCP, including its head, and the Chairman of the Republican Party began with showmanship. The CCP and Republican Party representatives attempted to bluff their way through the sessions. They showed no remorse for their actions. Their approach was aggressive in preaching the values of the United States and its history of being tolerant towards its enemies and nations who did it harm in some form. The committee representing the United States Government listened attentively, patiently. After several days of putting up with the hypocritical and blasphemous comments directed toward the President of the United States, the Democrats and members of the Freedom and Social Scientist Parties, the chairman representing the committee of the United States adjourned the session for one day.

On the second day of the meeting at Ft. McNair, the chairman of the group representing the United States opened the meeting with a peaceful tone. He proceeded to shock the CCP and Republican leaders present. He reviewed the history of the secession and the role of the CCP and Republican Party. He went

128

so far as to name the individuals and the roles they played in the action. He reminded them of who was responsible for the dramatic events that had occurred. The insult to the nation and the American people that the action brought. He reminded them of the impact that the secession had on the nation's prestige as a world leader. Many squirmed in their chairs but did not dare to leave the room. In leaving the room, they would lose any vestige of influence they might have on the final recommendations of the committee to the President and current leadership of the nation. They sat and listened to what could have been considered a presentation of the prosecution at a criminal trial.

Exactly two hours had passed in the opening comments. At the end, the chairman indicated that there would be no need for any further meetings of this group. The meeting was adjourned abruptly after the chairman indicated that the remarks presented by the CCP and Republican Party representatives the day prior would be noted and taken into account in their report and recommendations to the President of the United States.

The CCP and Republican Party leaders were in shock. They recouped quickly. They realized that the session could not end on the present note. There was no doubt that if they were to provide any semblance of assistance to New America, they would have to apologize to the chairman of the President's committee and admit their roles in creating an untenable situation for the United States. These proceedings were reported to the President of the United States that evening. He, in turn, briefed the leaders of the Freedom and Socialist Parties.

The committee representing the President of the United States scheduled a visit to Augusta, New America, to meet with that nation's President and his advisors. The meeting proved very fruitful.

The committee learned of the problems of New America. The economic picture presented to the committee revealed the seriousness of the conditions. The country had shortages in every conceivable consumer good. The nation had exhausted its supply of spare parts for farm equipment, cars, trucks, and other forms of transport including its ships and planes. Most vehicles could not be operated due to a lack of batteries, tires, and other essential products.

The lack of spare parts for farm equipment had an adverse impact on the agricultural industry. Fields could not be plowed and seeds could not be planted. Hence, there were few if any harvests. This caused food shortages throughout the new country. In addition, the export of agricultural products was non-existent.

The nation's factories, as few as there were, could not operate effectively. Spare parts and power were in short supply. The problem of unemployment was growing. Unrest of the citizens was noted.

The economy of New America was near collapse. This news was transmitted to the President of the United States. The committee requested guidance from the President. He sent word for the committee to return to Washington immediately.

Upon their return to Washington, the committee presented its findings to the President, the Congressional leaders, and the Chairmen of the Freedom and Socialist Parties. The presentation lasted three hours. At the end of this time, the committee was thanked for their efforts and excused. The meeting continued for another three hours. The plan was discussed and approved by those in attendance for the President of the United States to visit Augusta and to meet with the President of New America. The United States would extend an olive branch to the new nation. Economic aid would be offered without any preconditions if the President of New America so desired. The position taken by the President of the United States was that even though Maine and its citizens seceded from the United States, they were still considered Americans. For the most part, the majority of the people were the victims of the far right elements. The events were beyond their control. The suffering they were subjected to was not of their own doing.

The President of the United States visited Augusta as planned. His meeting with the President of New America was one on one. There were no staff members from either side present. The meeting took place in a private lodge located on the Atlantic coast. This site was selected at a moments notice to

130

preclude any wiring/recording to take place. The meeting was very amiable.

The two men reviewed the events of the past couple of years. At all times, they retained their composure and made every attempt to discuss the events and the current relationship rationally.

The President of the United States indicated that he had full knowledge of the economic problems of New America. He expressed his concern for the plight of the its citizens. The discussion also involved the stern policies of New America. The President did not hesitate to state his position on these issues. From his perspective, the strong stance taken against other political parties, unions, immigration and the abortion issue by New America contributed significantly to the economic problems of the country. The President of New America acknowledge that he, too, believed that many of the nation's problems could be directly attributed to these policies. This acknowledgment provided the President of the United States with the opening he sought.

The President of the United States suggested that if the official policies of New America would soften on the problem issues, the United States would be willing to extend aid to the country. The possibility of a loan that would permit the country to immediately start importing the necessary items to improve the nation's economy and the quality of life of its citizens was discussed.

Both men were aware of the sensitive position of the President of New America. His nation still had a hard core of citizens who belonged to the extreme right wing of the CCP and the Republican Party. He also knew that many were reporting to the leaders of both parties in the United States. Any quick action taken to soften the nation's stance on the critical issues could possibly open the doors to a military stand-off with the militias. As a result, both men agreed that the actions would be gradual and timed to preclude any radical actions on the part of the far right elements.

The time frame was developed that would remove all of the stringent controls within three years. This would give both men time to prepare for the conversion without causing any major ripples in the opposition.

The President of New America shocked the President of the United States when he offered two additional items to the timetable.

The President of New America indicated that he would schedule a plebiscite three years from the date of their meeting that would determine if the nation should remain independent or return to the United States as the State of Maine. If the people voted to remain independent, he would schedule national elections, open to all political parties within six months of the plebiscite. The President of New America indicated that he still believed in the issues he advocated for his country. However, he stated that he also recognized that the nation could not stand alone with its current philosophy in place.

The President of the United States accepted these comments with more than just relief. He indicated that he would immediately approve any aid that the President of New America would present to him at the earliest convenience. Both men shook hands and departed for their respective capitals.

There was no doubt the agreements arrived at during the short meeting would nurture the coexistence of the United States and New America.

EPILOGUE

The possibility of a State seceding from the Unite States is not as remote as some may believe. The United States has had episodes in its history that were unthinkable, but nevertheless they happened. The American Civil War was one episode in the nation's history that some, even today, find difficulty in accepting as a part of history. The civil disobedience actions that followed the assassination of the Reverend Martin Luther King were without precedent. Who would imagine that Washington, D.C., the nation's Capitol would be under siege. The city would be occupied by military troops. The steps of the nation's Capitol would have troops with mounted machine guns to protect the sacred building from rioters.

The immigration policies of the United States, particularly since the 1960's, resulted in millions of immigrants from every corner of the globe entering the country. People of all races, ethnic origin, and religious beliefs entered the nation in search of improving their quality of life and the lives of their descendents. This resulted in a myriad of back-grounds that make places like Bosnia, the African continent, and the Middle East look like a neighborhood in any of the country's metropolitan areas. There is no doubt that there will be clashes between and within these diverse groups. Hopefully, however, they will be contained and in due time become extinct. These people will learn to coexist just as the millions of immigrants who came from central Europe in the 19th and 20th centuries. That is America. This is what made the United States the strongest economic and military power in the history of the earth.

Finally, some may wonder why the writer selected the Christian Right, the Republican Party, and the specific issues in this book. After all, the United States is comprised of many people of color, religions, and ethnic backgrounds. If any people of color would attempt to plan and scheme an action that would cause a State to secede from the union, it would never succeed due to the awareness that group would cause by its actions.

Hence, the actions to accomplish secession by a Caucasian group would not be as obvious and not set off any alarms.

Besides, the Christian Right, the Republican Party, and the extreme right wing of both groups have demonstrated the ability to take such an action.

About the Author

Melvin R. Bielawski is a World War II veteran. In 1945-46 he was the American in charge of a hospital located in a German prisoner of war camp. Subsequent to his discharge from the Army, he attended the University of Toledo under the GI Bill and majored in industrial management. He received an MS in Public and Government Administration from George Washington University. A former resident of Toledo, Ohio, he and his wife currently reside in Alexandria, Virginia.

Mr. Bielawski retired from the Federal Civil Service. The Department of Defense, primarily the Army, employed him. Prior to his retirement from the Pentagon, he had various assignments with the Army including eight years in Germany. Subsequent to his departure from the Civil Service, he was self-employed as a consultant to industry and to the Government. He is currently fully retired and keeps active playing golf, fishing, traveling with his wife, and writing.

The Corner, written by Mr. Bielawski, has been donated to Florida State University together with the publication rights. He is currently writing another book dealing with his experiences in an American controlled German prisoner of war camp in the 1945-46 time frame.